OVERCOMERS

Gaining Victory Over the Obstacles in Life

JEFFREY BUSH

Our Generation Publishing
Alpharetta, GA
www.ourgenerationpublishing.com

Cover design by Nathaniel Bowman

Book Formatting by Chris Fies

For more copies, information, or questions, please check out ourgenerationpublishing.com or email me at jeff@ visionmissions.com

Table of Contents

Introduction

When I was growing up, I used the phrase "I can't" way too frequently. My dad would get on to me and tell me not to say those words. He would say that I could if I were willing to try hard enough. On more than one occasion, he said, "Say you won't, but don't say you can't!" It aggravated me. Why not just let me say it? But my dad knew something that took me years to figure out. You can if you try hard enough! You might not always want to do something, but you can do it, so quit using excuses. Saying the words "I can't" isn't convincing anyone that something can't be done. It's just a silly excuse to get out of doing it. My dad reminded me of this concept while playing sports, making money, learning at school, or working around the house. It was an attitude problem. My dad wasn't about to let me say, "I can't" because he knew I could.

And how much more does my Heavenly Father know and care for me! He never gives a task that is impossible or that cannot be accomplished without His help. Yet too many times, His children look up to Him and say, "I can't." If God is your God, you most certainly can! God's children are "more than conquerors through him that loved us." (Romans 8:37) This is much more than a cute phrase. It is a mantra for the Christian life: we are more than conquerors! Being a conqueror seeps into every aspect of life. There is nothing that a child of God cannot overcome. No longer can the devil defeat God's children. We must realize and live out being the overcomer He has destined us to be. Regardless of which bait the devil uses, God's children can overcome it. Depression, anger, bitterness, fear, sorrow, pride, or temptation has no power over a child of God. We are more than conquerors. We are overcomers!

As you open the pages of this book, you will be faced with real problems every person deals with on a daily basis. Too long have God's children thrown up the white flag. I don't pretend to have the knowledge or answers, but I do want to remind you of truths God has already given you. Stop saying you can't do it! You can overcome because you are an overcomer! God made you that way. It's more than positive-thinking, it's thinking the way God intended you to think. You are an overcomer, you can, and you must! Time to claim back the victory as a child of God.

Here to Serve,
Jeffrey Bush

Chapter 1

OVERCOMING FEAR

Fear is defined as "a painful emotion or passion excited by the expectation of evil or harm, and accompanied by a strong desire to escape it." If we were honest, all of us have some kind of fear. For a kid, it might be fear of the dark or of the boogie man. For the parent, it might be their children getting sick, becoming rebellious, or something bad happening to them. For the missionary, it might be fear of being accepted by the people, not learning the language, or starting the first church. For others, it might be fear of safety, sickness, fear for your kids, financial fear, failure, heights, snakes, spiders, robbery, or rejection from others.

It's interesting that statistics show the majority of things we fear are not real or even probable to happen. In other words, our minds make our fear look bigger and scarier than reality. I have heard and read many times that "F. E. A. R." is False Evidence Appearing Real. It's a mind game, yet it seems so real.

Fear is one of the areas that every person in the world struggles with, regardless of gender, age, marital status, financial status, or spiritual status. Yet as a Christian, we know the God of the Bible, and He has the answer for everything in life. So, let's run to God and see what His Word says about fear and how we can overcome it:

Realize you have a defender.

Every sport has a method of defense. A certain number of players will play defense so the opposing team does not score. Defenders are crucial in a game if the team is going to win. And in the game of life, we have God as our defender. So, whether your fear is about your future, the unknown, provision, or protection, just remember that you have a very big defender on your side—God. He's not just decent at His job, He is amazing at His job! With God on your side, there's no reason to fear!

Psalm 27:1-3 says, "The Lord is my light and my salvation; whom shall I fear? the Lord is the strength of my life; of whom shall I be afraid? When the wicked, even mine enemies and my foes, came upon me to eat up my flesh, they stumbled and fell. Though an host should encamp against me, my heart shall not fear: though war should rise against me, in this will I be confident."

When my kids were young and afraid at bedtime, we memorized and quoted Psalm 4:8, which says, "I will both lay me down in peace, and sleep: for thou, Lord, only makest me dwell in safety." With God as your defense, absolutely no one or nothing can break through. This is the defense that Daniel had when he slept in a pit with hungry lions. This is the defense Noah had when the floods rose up and destroyed the earth. This is the defense the three Hebrew children had when they were thrown in a fiery furnace. Neither wicked men, nor weapons, nor natural disasters, nor any other harm can get through our defense!

What are you afraid of? What is the thing that puts you into a panic and does not easily let you go? Think. Now compare that fear to your defense, and say the following: "What time I am afraid, I will trust in thee." Those were the exact words David used in Psalm 56:3. A portion of David's life was watching sheep alone at night while listening to the wolves howl and the lions roar. Another portion of his life was living in caves while King Saul persistently hunted him with intentions to kill him. The fear outside was dangerous and real, but the confidence within him cried out saying, "What time I am afraid, I will trust in thee." David's defense was bigger than his danger!

I love and highly recommend John Bunyan's classic, The Pilgrim's Progress. In the book, it talks about a narrow place along Christian's journey where two lions stood. Previously, others had turned back, and he was unsure of their reason, but now he was enlightened. At that moment, "The porter at the lodge, whose name is Watchful, perceiving that Christian made a halt as if he would go back, cried unto him, saying, 'Is thy strength so small? Fear not the lions, for they are chained, and are placed there for trial of faith where it is, and for discovery of those that had none. Keep in the midst of the path, no hurt shall come unto thee.' " The lions were big, but Christian's defense was bigger! And in the moments where you are walking through the valley of the shadow of death, you do not need to fear for God is with you (Psalm 23:4).

Understand that fear causes the heart to crumble.

Even though your fear may be legit, your fear doesn't change reality. In fact, your fear usually just worsens reality. Fear causes good people to stop attempting great things, hunker down, and become spiritually paralyzed. Fear is the absence of depending on God. In Deuteronomy 20:8, Moses commanded the officers to tell the soldiers that if any were fearful or fainthearted they should go home "lest his brethren's heart faint as well as his heart." Fear would not only cause a soldier's heart to crumble, it could also cause the entire army to fail. Fear is a nasty, contagious poison that destroys much of God's work.

God doesn't want His people to fear what man can do (Matthew 10:28). In fact, we are told that "the fear of man bringeth a snare" (Proverbs 29:25). A snare is a trap, and traps are used to catch animals. Some people may take the animal and release it, but most will kill the animal for food, leather, or just to get rid of it. Traps are not set to be loving or friendly; rather, they are set to expel and exterminate. You must realize that fear in your life is a snare that will both imprison and kill you.

We all know that faith comes by hearing (Romans 10:17), but fear also comes by hearing. Whether voices from within, from the news, or from others, you must be careful what you listen to and believe. News, social media, friends, and past experiences hold a proverbial megaphone in our hearts that cause us to panic, quit, and live in fear.

You remember the moment when Peter saw Jesus walking on the water and asked to join him? Jesus told Peter to step out of the boat. Peter got out of the boat and began walking on the water towards Jesus. What an experience! Then Peter looked around and saw the strong winds. He became afraid and began to sink. All was going well until he took his eyes off of Jesus and placed them on his surroundings. Fear almost cost him his life. Peter was wise enough to cry out for help, and Jesus extended His hand and saved Peter. Fear always tries to drown people, but it can be overcome by crying out to Jesus. Fear will rob you of joy. Fear causes you to lose God's blessings. Faith will keep you afloat, while fear tries to drown you. Let the Lord save you from drowning in fear by calling out to Him for help.

Know that God delivers from fear.

You may remember the time in the Bible when David went over to enemy territory for asylum. He had been chased by Saul far too long, and he was tired. Surely the enemies of his enemy would even out the score and give David a secure place to reside. When he arrived in front of King Abimelech (or Achish), the tables quickly turned and the Philistines remembered that David was the giant killer. David knew he was about to be captured and killed, so he began acting like a crazy man, letting spit go down his face and beard. Thankfully, Abimelech commanded his servants to kick out this crazy David as opposed to torturing and killing him. David escaped and wrote Psalm 34. He praised God, saying, "I sought the LORD, and he heard me, and delivered me from all my fears" (vs. 4). David was afraid, but the great fear-deliverer came through and rescued him. God is greater than any and every fear!

Paul told his young protégé, Timothy, that the spirit of fear did not come from God. In fact, God gives His children power, love, and a sound mind (2 Timothy 1:7). God does not cause fear, He delivers us from fear! The spirit of fear doesn't come from God, it comes from the enemy. Whenever fear strikes through your heart, remember that it's not God who is whispering it in your ears. Run to God, claim His promises, and know that He delivers His children from fear. Don't believe the lies of the devil, believe the truths from God! He has and will deliver you if you will just trust Him.

Learn to pray and wait on God.

Very few people are naturally patient, but it's easier to be patient when you know someone stronger, greater, and wiser than you has everything all under control. When you take something to God in prayer, you can be assured that He will take care of it. Even if it's outside the realm of your ability, finances, or understanding, it's not outside of God's. There is a peace that will flood over you when you take it to the Lord in prayer. Not only is there privilege in doing so, but there is great power on behalf of the One you're praying to. All your fears, worries, and woes can be taken to the One who is capable of handling anything you throw His way. It would do all of us good to think on and sing to ourselves the old hymn called "What A Friend We Have In Jesus" by Joseph M. Scriven:

O what peace we often forfeit
O what needless pain we bear
All because we do not carry
Everything to God in prayer!

The Psalmist said it perfectly when he said, "I had fainted, unless I had believed to see the goodness of the Lord in the land of the living" (Psalms 27:13). He finished out the same chapter by saying, "Wait on the Lord: be of good courage, and he shall strengthen thine heart: wait, I say, on the Lord." (Psalms 27:14) God will take care of you. Just take all your fears to Him and leave it with Him. There is no fear too small that should not be mentioned to Him, and there is no fear too big in which He cannot help.

Fear confuses reality.

I remember when I was young and still lived at my parents' house. It would be late at night, the lights would be off, and I was supposed to be going to sleep. I shared a room with my younger brother, who almost always drifted off to sleep before me. Although I wanted to go to sleep, I was awake and would be looking around the room. More than once, I was sure I saw someone else in the room. There was a clear outline of a person by the door or sometimes in front of the closet. I would put my head under the covers and try my hardest to go to sleep, fearful of whatever or whoever was in my room. Somehow I managed to go to sleep, only to wake up the next morning and see that my fear was nothing more than a shirt on a hanger. The light revealed my fear was in vain, but fear surely had me eaten up the night before. Even though this happened more than once, the boyish trick overtook me on too many nights. The fear wasn't reality, but it was enough to confuse reality. Far too often, fear continues clothing itself over skinny hangers in my adult life. I know the promises of God, statistics of something really happening, and clear facts, but fear always confuses reality.

I agree with Segun T. Obadimu when he says, "The right hand of the devil is fear." All truth we know is abolished, or at least utterly confused, when fear steps into the room. Obadimu also says, "To conquer the enemies in life, you must first conquer fear." When we are afraid, nothing else seems to make sense. According to the Bible, God is not the author of confusion (1 Corinthians 14:33). The devil wants to turn the lights out on what you know so he can take over making the shadows look like monsters. The child of God must turn on the light of God's Word, and fear will vanish immediately.

God says that perfect love casts out all fear (1 John 4:18). It's pretty easy to comprehend this concept when it comes to a friendship or marriage. If a wife was afraid of her husband, it would not be a good marriage. Well, if you are going to serve God, you have to kick out the fear or it will hinder you from serving Him. Whether you fear peer pressure, the uncertain future, where funds will come from, or protection from sickness and bad people, you have to kick fear to the curb. Love cannot and will not work where fear is present. Let me share an incident that happened to my family and I years ago:

We were still on the mission field living in Argentina. Petty theft happened frequently. Sound equipment, radio equipment, bikes, tools and various things had been stolen from both our church and house. We took precautions, but this time things escalated to a new level.

One Sunday night after a long weekend of ministry, we drove home from church, anticipating a nice, relaxing evening with the kids. We were walking into the house talking about our plans for the evening and which Andy Griffith show we were going to watch together. As Mindy closed the front door behind us, she felt someone pulling it back open from the outside. She let it go, thinking one of the kids must have still been outside.

Immediately, a gun was pointed at her, and two men barged into our house, yelled at us to get down on the floor, and waved their guns all around. My parents and nephew had just arrived from the States, so we had a house full of people. Thankfully, each of our girls was close enough to one of the adults as we were forced to sit down on the floor. The thieves demanded we give them money, cell phones, computers, and jewelry. One of them went over to my wife, reached out for her necklace, and tried to yank it off of her neck. She calmly told them to let her take it off. He asked for her wedding rings, which she had already taken off and slipped into her coat pocket. Not wanting to make them upset, she took them out and gave them to the thief.

The other thief took me upstairs to our bedroom and made me give him money that we had saved. He started dumping out stuff from drawers and closets in our room. He found our computers, and then emptied out my wife's jewelry box. During this time, my wife, my parents, and the kids were downstairs with the younger thief. He was no more than eighteen years old and seemed quite nervous. We wondered if it was his first robbery.

My wife took a quiet moment to ask him a few questions. "Are you going to kill us when you leave?" she asked him quietly, hoping the children wouldn't hear. He told her that they would not, and we did not need to worry. Somehow she believed him and went on questioning him. She asked if he believed in God and he said, "Yes."

She then told him, "Would you like to know the most valuable possession we own?" Of course he answered in the affirmative.

"See that book over there on the table?" she asked.

He went over, picked up her Bible and thumbed through it.

She told him that even if they killed us we knew we were going to Heaven, then she asked him if he knew.

When the other one brought me downstairs and made me sit again, he started to wave the gun around angrily wanting to know where I hid the "big money." They obviously thought they were going to get more than they did. He said that he was sent to our house because someone had been watching me take money out of the ATM and said we would have the church's offerings. I told him that the money went to the construction at the church. He didn't believe me so both of them started ransacking all the drawers and closets downstairs, stuffing things in their pockets every now and then.

They started to fill up my backpack with our computers, camera, cell phones, and money. The younger one started to put the Bible in the backpack and the other man told him, "Don't take that!" "But the lady gave it to me," he said, and stuffed it in the bag. It was very ironic considering they were just stealing everything around them, and now he acted like he needed to take it because it was a gift!

They found our passports, but when I asked him not to take them, he left them alone. I also asked him for a credit card that he had taken with some of the money, and he surprisingly gave it back. For a few minutes I was able to talk to him about the Lord and he listened, probably more so than the average person on the street! Finally, after more than an hour, they decided they weren't going to take anymore. The older one picked up some duct tape he had found in a drawer and was about to tie us up. I begged him to not touch my girls. Although it sounds crazy, he started to walk over to tie me up but then just set the tape down. I believe the Lord blinded his understanding as he just put the tape on the table and said, "Ok, let's go."

Before leaving, they ripped the phone out of the wall and said, pointing to our daughter Alexa, "If you report us to the police, we'll be back to take your daughter." As they walked out the door, Mindy jumped up and locked the door quickly. We looked at each other in amazement, having felt like we were finally at the end of a very bad dream. We all gathered together and through many tears, thanked the Lord for protecting us. Our nine-year-old daughter, Lydia, got her Bible and suggested we read a passage from Psalms.

Later my wife said, “Whenever I imagined that something like this would happen, I always imagined that we would all be hysterical and panicking, but somehow the Lord gave us all peace as if we were just calmly watching it happen in a dream.” Even our daughters were very calm when the men were in our house. Only once, towards the end, did they start to cry. And our VERY active 15-month-old, Alexa, somehow sat quietly on her Papaw’s lap for over an hour without moving! We knew God had protected us because many people have told us that usually when they come in unmasked, they kill so you cannot identify them. We believe that the Lord kept them from touching and harming us. (You can read more stories about robberies and God’s protection in our book *A Memoir of Miracles*.)

The days to follow were crucial ones. The robbery had already taken place, but now fear was more real than ever. It seemed like everyone we looked at could’ve been one of those thieves. Were they going to come back? Would they try to take my daughter? Would we ever be safe again? I remember a few long days thinking on it, and then sitting down to talk to my wife. I told her we could not live in fear and had to turn it over to the Lord. In no way do I want to oversimplify the matter, but God helped us get through it. The amazing thing was that 99% of the fear did not occur during the time the thieves were in our house. Instead, fear overwhelmed us the moment they left. It doesn't make logical sense that we would be more afraid of a thought than a real gun pointed in our faces, but that's how fear works. Fear confuses reality. It shuts the door on God and opens the door for the devil. If we will depend on God in our thoughts, letting His Word be the light in our darkness, the devil will be the one running for fear. Shed the light on fear by going to God. As the Psalmist David said, "The Lord is on my side; I will not fear: what can man do unto me?" (Psalm 118:6)

How appropriate are the powerful words of the old hymn "Living by Faith" written by James Wells:

> *Living By Faith, In Jesus Above,*
> *Trusting, Confiding In His Great Love;*
> *From All Harm Safe In His Sheltering Arm.*
> *I'm Living By Faith And Feel No Alarm.*

I once heard it is said that "fear not" is found 365 times in the Bible, one for every day of the week. Although I'm not positive on the exact number, it is certainly clear that God doesn't want any of His children to fear. As children of God, we can overcome the fear!

Let's close out this chapter meditating on one more great hymn entitled "Follow On." Read and meditate on the powerful words, and sing it to yourself silently or out loud if you know it.

> *Down in the valley with my Savior I will go,*
> *Where the storms are sweeping and the dark waters flow;*
> *With His hand to lead me I will never, never fear,*

Danger cannot fright me if my Lord is near.

Follow! Follow! I will follow Jesus!

Anywhere, everywhere, I will follow on!

Follow! Follow! I will follow Jesus!

Everywhere He leads me I will follow on!

Chapter 2

OVERCOMING PESSIMISM

Pessimism is a tendency to see the worst of things or believe the worst will happen. Pessimism is defeatism, negativity, doom and gloom, cynicism, hopelessness, depression, despair, or despondency.

In 2017, a Gallup poll said that 85% of people hate the job that they are currently doing. I do not believe that means most people need to change jobs, it probably means that most people need to change their attitude.

Being negative is more of a heart attitude than a personality issue. Your past problems, current circumstances, family flaws, or mishaps in life certainly affect your feelings, but they do not have to force you to become a negative person. The wisest man in the world, King Solomon, stressed for his son to "guard his heart," for from the heart is born every other issue (Proverbs 4:23). It's as if he says that criticism, condemnation, and confusion will be hurled your way from the outside, but you don't have to let them past the inner gates of your heart. You can daily build up the walls of your heart or restore the ones that are currently torn down. You don't have to blame your pessimism on your personality, circumstances, or past problems. You can decide to overcome the negativity and change. I pray this chapter will challenge you to rethink how you perceive life. If you're going to overcome pessimism, you should check out what God says about your attitude and decide to take His advice.

Understand the truth about complaining.

Allow me to ask you a couple of questions. Does God know you and your needs? Has God ever failed you in the past? Is God capable of providing for you? If you are a child of God, you already know the answer to these questions. Yet when you complain, essentially you are saying God doesn't take care of you. Complaining is not praising God. If anything, it's praising the devil. No child of God wants to give room for the devil to work, but complaining swings that door wide open and welcomes the devil to wreak havoc.

Immediately after the apostle Paul said that the Israelites had pushed God's buttons by complaining and were destroyed by serpents, he states that it was an example to give us instruction (1 Corinthians 10:10). Take heed. God doesn't like complaining. Complaining shows an attitude of ungratefulness and it seems to test God's patience. Later, in another letter, Paul said to do all without murmuring/complaining (Philippians 2:14). No parent wants to hear from their children that they're a lousy parent that can't or won't provide for them.

Neither does God delight in hearing His children complain about His care for them.

When you complain, you begin to focus on the negative and lose sight of all the good things. God has been good to you! If you were to get out a piece of paper right now and list the good things God has given you, two things would happen: First, you would realize how good you really have it. Second, you would quit being so pessimistic. In fact, you wouldn't have a reason to be negative. Your complaints make you and everyone else focus on the negative. Turn your complaining into praising!

Control your attitude.

You can't control the circumstances, but you can control your attitude. It's easy to pick up the victim mentality and become pessimistic. There are many reasons why things happen in life, but you must not forget that God likely wants to use the difficult moments to teach and grow you. You are commanded to have joy even when you face trials (James 1:2-4). Sadly, many people face hard times and become bitter, angry, depressed, or victimized. No matter what happens or has happened to you, you can allow those things to draw you closer to God instead of giving you a pessimistic attitude. Let God take control of your attitude instead of letting your attitude turn you into a negative person!

It would do you good to remember that the afflictions in life are momentary, not permanent (2 Corinthians 4:17). During difficult times God is working on the inside of you.

As was stated in the introduction, my dad used to get on to me whenever I would say, "I can't." He would tell me that I could if I tried. The problem wasn't my ability; it was my attitude. He would proceed to say, "You can say you won't, but don't say you can't." I needed to try harder. I needed to adjust my attitude. Looking back, I believe my dad understood much about life. Your attitude can push you forward or hold you back. Control your attitude before your negative attitude begins controlling you. But my dad isn't the only one who thinks this way. Our loving God tells His children they are more than conquerors (Romans 8:37), we can do all things through Him that strengthens us (Philippians 4:13), and that His promises are yea, and in Him, Amen (2 Corinthians 1:20). There is no need to become stressed or negative when you have those promises! God's promises don't change. What needs to change is our attitude and dependence on His promises!

Place the right influence around you.

One of my favorite books is Rhinoceros Success by Scott Alexander. One of the many good pieces of advice this book offers is that you become the product of three things: the books you read, the people you associate with, and the media you listen to. The wise King Solomon said if you walk with wise men you will be wise (Proverbs 13:20). In other words, whatever or whoever you allow to influence you will end up forming you. If you are going to overcome pessimism, you have to place the right influence in your life. Let's run through some influences that will steer you from negativity and gear you to positivity:

1. You need God's Word. This is more than the typical Christian answer. God's Word will help you fix your eyes on the future instead of fretting about the present. The Christian that goes days without reading the Bible is starving himself while God has a banquet prepared before him. The Bible is a mirror upon which you can check your desires, priorities, and attitude. The Bible will give you the right perspective on life. The Bible is the positive influence you need. Don't starve yourself. You need the Bible!

2. You need people who will lift you up. You certainly need to be a witness to the lost, a friend to your spiritual brothers, and an example to all; but you should also avoid the complainers, criticizers, mean spirited, and negative people until they change. They will affect your spirit. They'll suck the joy right out of you. Proverbs 13:20 teaches that if you walk with wise men, you will be wise. Do you want to overcome pessimism? Don't hang out with the pessimistic!

3. You need to change your thoughts. It sounds simple, but when it comes down to it, that's exactly what you have to do. Start thinking about what God thinks of you instead of what you were told or how you feel about yourself. Remember that God says you are accepted in the beloved (Ephesians 1:6). God tells you to check out what is true, honest, just, pure, lovely, and of good report, and to think on these things (Philippians 4:8). You should

stop right now and ask yourself where your thoughts are coming from. If they're not from God, they're from the enemy. Time to reconsider and rethink!

Count your blessings.

When was the last time you stopped and counted your blessings? If you are a pessimistic person, you most likely have to admit that you haven't done it recently. If you do count your blessings, you will realize you have less to fuss about and more for which to thank God. Don't stop at just counting your blessings; write down your blessings and repeat them to God. Counting your blessings, writing them down, and rehearsing them back to God will change your perception on life.

God tells us that we don't have to worry, stress, or be anxious about anything ("be careful for nothing"), because we can take it all to Him in prayer (Philippians 4:6). Knowing that God hears our prayers and cares for us is a beautiful truth. The Master and Creator of the universe takes time to bend His ear to mere mortals like us. But sometimes we forget that in that same portion of Scripture mentioned prior, we are told to let our requests be known "with thanksgiving." We might obey by taking all to God in prayer (though I fear we often neglect this basic truth), but we must not forget to do so "with thanksgiving." Start your prayers by praising God, and your mood and focus will soon change from negativity to positivity.

Listen to the words God offers in Lamentations 3:21-24: "This I recall to my mind, therefore have I hope. It is of the Lord's mercies that we are not consumed, because his compassions fail not. They are new every morning: great is thy faithfulness. The Lord is my portion, saith my soul; therefore will I hope in him." If you were to let your mind marinate in verses like this, you would soon cease from dwelling on the negative. Pessimism stems from a wrong focus.

Allow me to finish this chapter by reminding you that Moses sent twelve men to spy out the promised land. God had already promised Israel they were going to possess a land of milk and honey. Moses sent one man from each tribe to check it out before the great conquest. When they returned, only two of the twelve believed they could conquer this land. Ten of the twelve, or 83%, said that the task was impossible. Soon their lack of faith and pessimistic attitudes caused them to lose out on God's blessing and be stuck in the desert for forty years. They had the promise, and had seen God's protection and provision, but they didn't believe God would really do what He said He would do. And there are way too many times that God's children repeat this same pessimistic attitude and end up losing out on God's blessings. This attitude is nothing more than a lack of faith. Oh dear friend, change your attitude from looking at your surroundings to looking to God. The giants are big compared to you, but they are small compared to your God. Believe God, and let your attitude reflect that belief. Below are two final verses to meditate on before we end this lesson on pessimism.

John 10:10 — "The thief cometh not, but for to steal, and to kill, and to destroy: I am come that they might have life, and that they might have it more abundantly."

Romans 15:13 — "Now the God of hope fill you with all joy and peace in believing, that ye may abound in hope, through the power of the Holy Ghost."

Let's conclude this chapter thinking on an old hymn entitled "Count Your Blessings." The song seems to deal with the heart attitude. Sing it to yourself if you know it, whether silently or out loud, and I'm certain your attitude will go from negative to positive.

Are you ever burdened with a load of care?
Does the cross seem heavy you are called to bear?
Count your many blessings, every doubt will fly,
And you will keep singing as the days go by.
Count your blessings, name them one by one.
Count your blessings, see what God hath done.
Count your blessings, name them one by one;
And it will surprise you what the Lord hath done.

Chapter 3

OVERCOMING GRIEF

Grief can be considered a deep sorrow, misery, sadness, anguish, pain, distress, agony, torment, affliction, suffering, heartache, heart-break, broken-heartedness, or heaviness of heart.

There are many reasons for which grief enters into one's life. The following are a few reasons that you or someone you know may face grief: loss of a loved one, loss of a job, being criticized or spoken about negatively by someone else, sickness of a loved one, or tragedy in your life or the life of someone you love. Grief is no respecter of persons and seems to creep its way into the life of almost everyone at some point in time. Although some problems or situations can be avoided, grief usually sneaks in without permission and tends to stays longer than one desires. We cannot avoid all the circumstances that bring grief, but we can learn to overcome grief by using God's principles.

I'll never forget the day my wife and I went to the hospital to find out the gender of our newest baby. We were living in Argentina and my wife was four months pregnant. It was finally time for the doctor to tell us if we were going to have a boy or girl. God had already given us three precious girls and we were excited to find out what our next gift from God was going to be. We made our way from the waiting room to the doctor's office, where my wife sat on the table. The doctor began using a sonogram scanner on my wife's stomach to take pictures of the baby. After a few attempts, the doctor left the room and came in with another doctor. Within minutes, a few other doctors came into the room, and we knew something was not right. My wife began crying and I was trying to console her, letting her know all would be just fine. But things weren't fine. The doctor finally broke the news to us that our precious child was dead in the womb. The unwanted visitor of grief struck our household that day and stayed with us for a long time.

Grief sometimes has a way of trampling people to a point at which they no longer believe or want anything to do with God. Too many times I've witnessed people go through grief and become bitter at God instead of growing and drawing closer to God. When grief strikes, it may not always be understood and certainly not welcomed, but as a Christian, we can run to God's Word and research some truths for times of grief.

God works all things for our good.

Listen to the promise of Romans 8:28: "And we know that all things work together for good to them that love God, to them who are the called according to his purpose." Do you love God? Well, according to this verse, God can use even the bad for your good. Grief may look like an ugly frog, but God might just have plans to turn it into a handsome prince. It might not make sense to you now, or ever, but somewhere inside of this bad situation, God has plans to use it for your good and for His glory.

Before we can move on, you have to get this fact straight. Nothing surprises God or can happen without His knowledge. Your loving God wants to do something even in the midst of this nasty storm you are going through. Don't lose hope; your rock and refuge is God. Your hope is not in another person or in your own ability to manage the situation. Rest assured that God knows best, and He can make this work for good.

But what about a loved one that died? Why? What about a crippling or even fatal illness? Why? Dear friend, I do not know why God allows certain things, but I do know that you can take His promises to the bank and He said that ALL things are going to work together for good, not for bad. God knows better and has a plan through it all. You will never understand everything, but you can understand that God knows best.

I love the words that our Lord gave to Israel in Isaiah 43:2: "When thou passest through the waters, I will be with thee; and through the rivers, they shall not overflow thee: when thou walkest through the fire, thou shalt not be burned; neither shall the flame kindle upon thee." And the words that the suffering servant of God, Job, said in Job 23:10: "But he knoweth the way that I take: when he hath tried me, I shall come forth as gold." You see, God might allow you to go through some hard times, but God has a plan and a purpose.

If you lost a loved one that was saved, know that you will see them in Heaven.

Paul told the believers in Thessalonica that they didn't have to be ignorant concerning the death of a child of God. In fact, they didn't have to sorrow "as others which have no hope" (1 Thessalonians 4:13). Certainly, it hurts when we lose a loved one, but we can know they're not lost or gone forever. They are with the Lord. For a child of God, their last breath upon the earth is their first breath in Heaven (Philippians 1:23). There is no purgatory, soul sleep, or waiting period for a child of God. "To be absent from the body is to be present with the Lord" (2 Corinthians 5:8).

The Psalmist says it pretty straightforwardly: "Precious in the sight of the Lord is the death of his saints" (Psalm 116:15). It is painful in our eyes to have a loved one die, but to God, it is precious. Grief doesn't have to overcome us as God's children.

God doesn't abandon us. He hears us.

Grief has a way of making us think that God is far from us, but that is not the case at all. Psalm 34:18 says, "The Lord is nigh unto them that are of a broken heart; and saveth such as be of a contrite spirit." God has not abandoned you. If we were to run through the Word of God, we know well that God doesn't abandon His children. He has promised to never leave us nor forsake us (Hebrews 13:5). He has a perfect track record, and you can definitely count on Him! Don't allow your feelings to deceive you into doubting Him.

In Psalm 31, David is going through a pretty bad time. In verse nine he says, "Have mercy upon me, O Lord, for I am in trouble: mine eye is consumed with grief," and in verse ten, he says, "My life is spent with grief." It's pretty obvious he is grieving. Grief seems to have almost swallowed him up. In the verses to follow, he confesses his trust is in God, but the conclusion of the chapter changes the tune of all when it says, "Be of good courage, and he shall strengthen your heart, all ye that hope in the Lord" (vs. 24). It seems that David says, "Cheer up, he hasn't left you and doesn't plan on it." God will lift and strengthen your heart, so hope in Him and cheer up. God hasn't abandoned you and He never will!

God is our comforter.

Our God has many titles, but one of the many assuring ones in difficult times is the title He is given in 2 Corinthians 1:3, "the Father of mercies, and the God of all comfort." No matter what pain and grief you are going through, never forget that you have a Comforter!

Our Jesus told His disciples in John 14 that He would be leaving and going back to Heaven with His Father. But he told them to not worry because He was going to leave them a Comforter that would be with them forever (John 14:16). The Holy Spirit, Whom Christ was presenting and promising them, is Who we now have living and abiding in us Christians today (Ephesians 1:13; 4:30). He is forever with us, and He is our Comforter!

It is okay to grieve.

It's not wrong to grieve, but you must allow God to use the grief in your life to cause you to turn to Him. Grieving is not wrong. Of course, you miss the loved one that is no longer with you. The question is, will you choose to allow the grief to fuel you or anchor you down? Allow me to explain. Grief can push you to look to God, to love those who are still with you, to use your time more conscientiously, and to be more open and expressive to others on a constant basis. The negative side would be that grief can cause you to withdraw from everyone, blame God, become angry at the world, and not want to continue living. Although it may seem painful, you must decide to allow God to use the difficult moments in your life for your good and for His glory. So, yes, do grieve, but allow the end of that grief to cause you to run to the Lord instead of run from the Lord.

Before we leave this subject, allow me to tell you that not only can God help you overcome the grief in your own life, but it might just be that God wants to use you to help someone else through their grief. Pay close attention to what it says in 2 Corinthians 1:3-4: "Blessed be God, even the Father of our Lord Jesus Christ, the Father of mercies, and the God of all comfort; Who comforteth us in all our tribulation, that we may be able to comfort them which are in any trouble, by the comfort wherewith we ourselves are comforted of God." Did you notice that? God has full intentions for you to learn from being comforted so that you can turn around and comfort others. Don't let the hard time you are going through discourage you. Allow God to use it in your life so you can minister to others.

One last word of encouragement from King David, the sweet Psalmist of Israel, in Psalm 119:50: "This is my comfort in my affliction: for thy word hath quickened me." You can run to God and His Word in your hard times and grieving moments, for He is your comfort!

Let's close out this chapter meditating on the old hymn entitled "Farther Along." The song offers both a question and an answer, explaining even the timing to our understanding.

> *Often I wonder why I must journey*
> *Over a road so rugged and steep;*
> *While there are others living in comfort,*
> *While with the lost I labor and weep.*
> *Farther along we'll know more about it.*
> *Farther along we'll understand why;*

Cheer up my brother live in the sunshine

We'll understand it all by and by.

Chapter 4

OVERCOMING TEMPTATION

According to the dictionary, a temptation is "the desire to do something, especially something wrong or unwise." Since the beginning of time, temptations have existed. Eve was tempted to ignore God and fulfill her own desires. Not much has changed since then. This world is full of temptations. Whether the temptation is pornography, discouragement, hatred, unfaithfulness, fear, or failure, absolutely any temptation can be overcome because God's children are overcomers. Let's study about what God says considering temptation and how we can overcome it in our own lives.

Temptations are common to everyone.

The tendency is to think that you are the only one who has these temptations, and as a result, no one can really understand you or your situation. According to God, this is not true. 1 Corinthians 10:13 says, "There hath no temptation taken you but such as is common to man." In other words, you are not the only one who deals with temptations, regardless of the temptation. Let's take a peek at a few people in the Bible who were tempted:

1. Joseph: In Genesis 39:7, Joseph's master's wife was after him so much that she asked him to sleep with her. Although the Bible doesn't go into detail, this was a pretty hot pursuit for sexual desire. Potiphar was one of the richest and most powerful men alive, meaning his wife was probably not ugly. Joseph was minding his own business and trying to do right, yet this temptation for sexual seduction was in his face, sought him out, and was available if he wanted it.

2. Balaam: In Numbers 22:17, Balaam was offered promotion and riches if he would just curse God's people. Balaam was God's servant, but the king came to him and offered a truckload of treasures if he would say a few quick words against God's people. Just turn his back once and the riches would all be his. Couldn't he later say that he didn't mean it? Couldn't he have acted like he said it? It's just a few words. Seems pretty tempting.

3. Achan: In Joshua 7:21, Achan was on soldier duty when he saw the riches in one of the enemy's tents. Would anyone know or even blame him if he just kept a little for himself? It looked so good, and the forbidden treasure seemed to almost jump into his arms. The temptation was so strong that he decided to give into it.

4. David: In 2 Samuel 11:2, David saw Bathsheba bathing and she was "very beautiful to look upon." Was it really his fault that she was out there? He's the king, so doesn't he deserve a little pleasure if he wants it? Nobody would really know, would they? The glance became a stare, the stare became a desire, and the desire became a reality.

We could mention Jeroboam, who was tempted to follow his heart (1 Kings 15:30); Peter, who denied Christ because he was afraid (Mark 14:67-71); or our Lord Jesus, who was hungry after fasting and subsequently tempted by the devil (Matthew 4). The point is that temptations flaunted themselves in front of Bible heroes, as well as our Lord, and they will certainly not put the brakes on for you or me today. Remember what God said, "There hath no temptation taken you but such as is common to man" (1 Corinthians 10:13). This does not mean that temptations are a good thing, rather that they are something that happens in the life of every person. You are not the only one who has temptations. It's easy to think that no one struggles with temptations like you do, but this is a lie from the devil. Regardless of the financial status, age, education, or position you hold in a church, temptations are going to present themselves to you. The verse goes on to say, "But God is faithful, who will not suffer you to be tempted above that ye are able; but will with the temptation also make a way to escape, that ye may be able to bear it." Although temptations might be common to all mankind, God can help you overcome the temptations!

Understand the breeding grounds for temptations.

Although temptations are "common to man," we must realize that temptations are usually born and definitely fueled by our own lusts. Listen to the words in James 1:13-14: "Let no man say when he is tempted, I am tempted of God: for God cannot be tempted with evil, neither tempteth he any man: But every man is tempted, when he is drawn away of his own lust, and enticed."

God tells us that temptations do not come from Him, but from our own lust. Lust is a passionate desire for something, specifically sexual desire. Here's two examples: someone is tempted to consume alcohol or drugs because his friends are doing the same, or because it's in his house. Or he might be tempted to look at pornography because it popped up on the phone and with one click he can see much more. The point is that the temptations flare up when the door is opened by foolish decisions. James 1 gives the idea that God is saying, "Don't you try to pin this one on me. You fell into those temptations because you were in the wrong place, with the wrong people, or you let the wrong influence linger too long before closing the door." Because someone is angry, they are tempted to say hurtful things to others. Because someone is not satisfied with what God has given them, they are tempted to covet what others have. Whether coveting someone's money, spouse, car, house, or life, the temptation is not from God, but rather a manifestation of dissatisfaction with God and His provision. According to Matthew 4:3 and 1 Thessalonians 3:5, one of the devil's names is "the tempter." The temptations are not coming from God, they are coming from the tempter, the devil!

There are consequences to giving in to temptation.

Peter Marshall, a Scottish-American preacher greatly used by God as chaplain in the US Senate, said in A Man Called Peter, "It's no sin to be tempted. It isn't the fact of having temptations that should cause us shame, but what we do with them." Think about King David from the Bible. As he walked on the roof, he saw Bathsheba bathing. The problem came about when he gave into the temptation and called her to his house. Temptations seem to be ever-present. But temptations are not necessarily the problem; what we do with the temptation is the problem. Whether something seen on a screen, a thought that pops into one's mind, or suggestive offers that are not sought out, temptations are going to present themselves at some point. It is the yielding to the temptation that brings the consequences. If you were to ask someone if they want to destroy their marriage, ruin their testimony, hurt those they care about, or not be trusted again, the obvious answers would be "no." But giving into the temptations always ends in destruction. First John 2:17 offers the needed answer: "And the world passeth away, and the lust thereof: but he that doeth the will of God abideth for ever." The temptations that we think will please us are short-lived and unfulfilling. One day those pleasures will blow away with the wind. The answer lies in doing the will of God. Serving God today means saying no to that temptation, and the same goes for tomorrow and the next day. In the end, serving God, and doing His will, is what really lasts. The consequences of yielding to temptations are grave, but rejecting them to serve the Savior brings lasting pleasure.

Take Biblical steps to resist and overcome temptation.

In 2 Peter 2:9, we see that "the Lord knoweth how to deliver the godly out of temptations." What a beautiful truth to know that God can and will deliver us from temptations. So let's check out some of the tools God provides in His Word to help us resist and overcome temptation:

By faith. After 1 Peter 5:8 tells us that the devil is a roaring lion (not a cuddly kitty cat) that wants to destroy and devour, God then tells us in the next verse to "resist (him) stedfast in the faith." Faith is what we can't see but what we hope in because God has told us it is so. Faith is knowing that God can deliver us and that we can resist temptation firmly and continually. Ephesians 6:16 tells us to hold up the shield of faith. How long do you hold up a shield? As long as you're fighting! Hold that shield of faith high because the devil is hurling fiery darts of temptation your way.

Avoid It. Proverbs 4:15 gives us the instruction by saying, "Avoid it, pass not by it, turn from it, and pass away." If you know there's something that can take you down, then be smart and run. You might have been told that a tough man doesn't run, but a wise man does run when it comes to temptation. Don't stick around and find out how strong you are, get out of there. When warning about sexual sins, Proverbs 5:8 suggests to not even get close to the doorstep, but to remove yourself far from there. If the temptation is avoided, there's not much of a chance of falling. If you stay in the line of fire, you will most likely be shot. The apostle Peter gave sound advice to abstain from anything that wars against your soul (1 Peter 2:11). Don't mess with it. Avoid it!

Yield yourself and your members to God. In Romans 6, God's children are told to yield (relinquish, hand over, surrender) themselves and the members of their bodies to God. If the hands, feet, eyes, or mouth belong to God, then don't surrender them to the devil for unrighteousness. God reminds us that one is slave to that which he yields himself. So, be honest and ask yourself, do you want to be a slave to alcohol, anger, fornication, bitterness, or pornography? Or do you want to be God's servant? If you want to overcome temptation, make sure you don't yield yourself, or the members of your body, to temptation.

Deny yourself. In Matthew 16:24, Jesus said to His disciples, "If any man will come after me, let him deny himself, and take up his cross, and follow me." You must decide who you are going to please, Christ or yourself. Self wants to be fulfilled and have it all now, but you must learn to say "no" to self so you can say "yes" to God. If you can't say "no" to your desires, you can't say "yes" to His desires. The apostle Paul said, "I die daily" (1 Corinthians 15:31). Daily, a child of God must say no to self-fulfillment so He can keep God first and foremost in his life. Self-denial requires discipline, but it shows the flesh, the world, and the devil Who is the priority in your life.

Replace it. There is a principle throughout the Word of God that teaches God's children to put off certain things and put on other things. The following verses all teach this principle: James 1:21, 1 Peter 2:1-2, Ephesians 4:22-25, Colossians 3:8-14, and Romans 13:12-14. Yes, you should stop doing whatever it is that is causing you to fall prey to the devil's grips, but you should replace it with good things so you are no longer vulnerable. For example, if hanging around certain people is the segue to doing something you regret, then change up your friends. If being alone at certain times of the day is when your temptation is strongest, then set up some accountability with someone to report your actions to during that time. Pinpoint your place, time, or reason for stronger temptations. Then replace that with another activity. Don't allow the devil to win the battle. You can put off the bad and put on the good. As a result you'll overcome the temptation that has held you captive for too long.

Refer to His Word. In Matthew 4, when the devil is tempting Jesus, the Lord replies to each of the devil's temptations with the same words: "It is written" (vs. 4,7,10). Instead of disputing, Jesus simply reminded the devil about the unchanging agent of God's Word. While everything in this world is wavering, God's Word is already settled in Heaven (Psalm 119:89). If our Lord referred to God's Word, we would be wise to do the same. Remind the devil what God says. The Psalmist David said to hide God's Word in your heart to not sin against Him (Psalm 119:11). In moments of strong temptation, sing yourself a song about truth from God's Word or quote a passage from it. Our strength is no match for the devil and his temptations, but refer to God's Word and you'll send him scurrying down the road.

Cry out to God. In Matthew 6:9, the Lord begins to explain how to pray, and in verse 13 it says, "Lead us not into temptation, but deliver us from evil." It always feels better when you can talk to someone about your struggle, and God says He wants to be that person. You don't have to go through temptation after temptation alone, you can talk to God! While that sounds like a cliché, it's not. Hebrews 2:18 says, "For in that he himself hath suffered being tempted, he is able to succour them that are tempted." Our Savior knows what temptation is, He was tempted, passed the test, and can help you in your temptations. The next time you are tempted, ask God aloud to help you and give you strength. Remind yourself that He will not leave nor forsake you. You belong to Him, He purchased you, and He wants the best for you. As you talk to God, the temptation will begin to lose its appeal, and you will more successfully walk away from the temptation.

Wake up and watch. In Matthew 26:41, Jesus said, "Watch and pray, that ye enter not into temptation: the spirit indeed is willing, but the flesh is weak." Jesus had been telling His disciples to pray with Him, but they kept falling asleep. They were tired, but Jesus was talking about something deeper. He continued to tell them to watch (vs. 38,40,41), but they continued falling asleep. And spiritually, too many Christians are sleeping (Romans 13:11; 1 Corinthians 15:34). We are told to wake up because the time is short and the devil is astute. Wake up and be alert. Realize that temptation might look good but will leave you empty. Realize that sin has consequences. Realize that the devil wants to destroy you. Wake up and don't let the temptation steal the joy you have for Jesus. Watch and don't mindlessly sleep while the devil works to destroy your life. Temptation is about pleasing self. Wake up and kick self off the throne. Wake up and watch lest you dethrone God from the throne of your life.

Remember your identity. When the devil tempted Jesus in Matthew 4, he attacked the identity of Jesus, saying, "If thou be the Son of God" (vs. 3,6). Of course, He was the Son of God. All the temptations of the devil are attacks against the identity of Christ. Jesus replied saying, "Thou shalt not tempt the Lord thy God" (vs. 7). The devil attacked His identity, but Jesus didn't let the devil forget His identity. In his book Tempted and Tried, Russell Moore says, "Temptation is so strong in our lives precisely because it's not about us. Temptation is an assault by the demonic powers on the rival empire of the Messiah." The devil's attacks are against God, so if the devil can cause you to doubt your identity in God, he wins the battle. Every child of God must remember that in the dark and doubting moments of temptation, his identity is "hid with Christ in God" (Colossians 3:3). Your victory is in your identity. You are a child of God! You are more than a conqueror! You are an overcomer! Don't forget your identity!

Check out a beautiful promise from God. James 1:12 says, "Blessed is the man that endureth temptation: for when he is tried, he shall receive the crown of life, which the Lord hath promised to them that love him." More than the rewards received for enduring temptations,

I want you to see that it is possible to endure the temptation. There is nothing impossible for God, so as God's child, run to Him and allow Him to help you endure and overcome the temptations!

Let's close out this chapter meditating on the old hymn entitled "Yield Not to Temptation." The song offers great advice and truth when it comes to the area of temptation.

Yield not to temptation, for yielding is sin;
Each vict'ry will help you some other to win;
Fight manfully onward, dark passions subdue;
Look ever to Jesus, He'll carry you through.
Ask the Savior to help you,
Comfort, strengthen, and keep you;
He is willing to aid you,
He will carry you through.

Chapter 5

OVERCOMING ANGER

I remember specifically an anger outrage I had one time as I was driving down the interstate. Another driver and I had been recklessly taunting each other. As the anger culminated, the other driver furiously motioned me to pull over. Within seconds, both of our vehicles cut across multiple lanes to the shoulder of the interstate. Before I could stop my vehicle, the other driver had thrown open his door, put his black SUV in park, and was reaching under his seat to grab something. Whether a bat or gun, I wasn't about to stick around and find out. Fear and reality smashed together as I sped off as quickly as possible. My countenance and attitude changed, and now I was repentant. I prayed God would forgive my anger and save me from my stupidity. What started off as being a cut off and honking back and forth morphed into an angry rage that almost got me killed.

You may have never sunk as low as I did in the previous story, but you can probably remember a moment when your anger caused you to say hurtful words or carry out hurtful actions. Anger is a faulty bomb that has destroyed many marriages, families, churches, and individuals. Anger is almost always self-absorbed and destroys anything in its path, leaving the beholder empty and depressed in the aftermath.

I remember in recent years hearing about a pastor's wife killing her husband with a shotgun because she was so angry at how he treated her. Another real incident was about an angry student at a university in Virginia that had enough bullying and ended up killing several students with two semi-automatic weapons. Other incidents include road rage, parents who couldn't handle their children, lover's disputes, and anti-government groups. Anger has risen so high that even news channels have spoken about it multiple times. The end result of anger is ugly. In cartoons or comic book characters such as the Incredible Hulk, the "normal" man is changed when he gets angry, and the anger causes mass destruction.

At times, my wife has asked me if I'm angry about something. To not appear so dramatic, I sometimes tell her, "No, I'm not angry, I'm just upset." I have used other synonyms such as "disappointed," "aggravated," "hurt," or "perturbed." I might think I'm fooling my wife by using different words, but the blunt truth is that I'm not tricking anyone. Yes, there might be levels of anger, but the results are damaging either way. A few ramifications of anger are marriages torn apart, children hurt, jobs lost, friendships ended, and bitterness taking root in the life of everyone involved. God teaches in Proverbs 14:17, "He that is soon angry dealeth foolishly." Anger destroys almost all those it touches, and is proven a foolish way of dealing with life.

In the book of Proverbs, we are told that a person who is able to control his anger is better than a mighty man (Proverbs 16:32). Think of the coolest Navy Seal you can imagine. God says if you can control your anger, you're even stronger and greater than that guy. If you have always wanted to be a tough guy, now is your chance! God commands us to "cease from anger" (Psalms 37:8), because "anger resteth in the bosom of fools" (Ecclesiastes 7:9). So here's your choice: would you rather be the mighty man or the fool? God lays it out rather clearly, but He also lets you make your own choice. You might say, "I can't help it. It's beyond my control." While you may have had bad examples in your past or created bad habits on your own, you can still overcome your anger. Let's take a look at some ways you can overcome your anger:

Recognize what God says about anger.

As we begin our journey on overcoming anger, first consult God's opinion on the subject. If you are a child of God, you desire to please Him, and as a result, knowing His thoughts on a matter is important to you. You might say, "Yeah, I already know He doesn't like my anger," but I'm convinced you really do care what God thinks. If you love someone, you want to please that person, so getting God's scoop on the matter of anger should be important to you. So let's take a quick look — not to condemn, but rather to understand.

First, we see that anger doesn't work the righteousness of God (James 1:20). I think you would agree that over 90% of the times you get angry, the results are not pleasing to God. Many like to use the example of Jesus turning over the money tables, but let's be honest, most of us are not exactly thinking of God when we get angry. The words we use when we get angry, the raised voice, or the thoughts considered during a moment of anger are not working the righteousness of God. In fact, God says when someone is quick to get angry, he only glorifies foolishness (Proverbs 14:29). God wants to be the One glorified, but our anger makes that impossible. Until you accept the fact that your anger is hurting others and poorly representing God, you will not overcome this problem.

No one can make you angry; you choose to get angry. Let that sink in: anger is a choice that you make. It cannot be forced on you. It is important that you understand this. Recognize that your anger is crippling you from growing, and it is hindering relationships and opportunities God has for you. God has much more for you, so don't let your anger keep you from that!

Respect the Spirit of God.

Who runs your life? Do your actions and reactions reveal that God's Spirit runs your life? It might be a hard pill to swallow, but if you could watch your life like a movie, would you say that your behavior lines up with your beliefs? Ephesians 5:18 teaches that God's children should be filled and controlled by the Spirit of God, and Galatians 5:22-23 shares the fruit that will be produced when one is filled with the Spirit. Anger is not in the list. In fact, almost every characteristic mentioned is the polar opposite of anger.

Did you know that we can actually sadden the Holy Spirit? Ephesians 4:30 commands us to not grieve the Holy Spirit. The verse before (vs. 29) talks about not letting corrupt speech proceed from your mouth, and the verse after (vs. 31) talks about putting anger away from you. Your actions and attitude can sadden the Holy Spirit, so God says to put those things off. God's children should respect God's Spirit, not sorrow Him.

Respond by turning anger into love.

In Romans 12:21, God says, "Be not overcome of evil, but overcome evil with good." God wants your anger turned into love. Someone may have offended, hurt, criticized, or cheated you, but God commands you to overcome that evil with love. It's easy to love those that love you, but God teaches to love them that don't love you, the ones that do you wrong (Matthew 5:43-48). Instead of saying, "I'm better than I used to be; you should have known me before," God wants you to be like Him. You can transform that anger into love by letting God be your filter, your example, and your motivation. You can learn to act instead of react. God says to put away from you the anger (Colossians 3:8) and instead, to be kind, tenderhearted, and forgiving (Ephesians 4:31-32). God's answer is to love through forgiveness and kindness. Respond like Christ responds!

Remember to clear accounts daily.

In Ephesians 4:26-27, we are commanded to not let the sun go down upon our wrath. You don't have to be a scientist to know the sun rises every morning and sets every evening. God clearly states that before the sun sets, He wants you to clean the slate so the devil will not have room to work.

The devil is our enemy. He is the thief that comes to steal, kill, and destroy (John 10:10). No one in their right mind leaves the door open or unlocked if they know there's a thief in the neighborhood, yet that is exactly what you do every time you don't forgive before the sun goes down. God tells us to not be ignorant of the devil's devices because he will certainly take advantage of them (2 Corinthians 2:10:11). In the context of that verse, God says that Satan's taking advantage has to do with forgiveness. If you become angry and don't forgive, the devil will take advantage, and you will not like the results daily. God loves you and doesn't want you to become prey to the devil, so clear all accounts. When the account is emptied daily, you don't have to worry about bitterness setting in and exploding the next time you see that person. One of Satan's clever tools for taking advantage of God's children is bitterness. Clear the account daily by forgiving others so bitterness will not take root, and the devil will not have room to work.

Check out this verse concerning some of God's characteristics. Psalms 145:8 says, "The Lord is gracious, and full of compassion; slow to anger, and of great mercy." If anyone has ever been wronged, it is God. God created the world, yet the world denies and ignores Him. Even so, our God is still "slow to anger, and of great mercy." We have a perfect and constant example in our Lord, now let us overcome anger in our own lives and represent our Lord well.

A list of a few more helpful verses on the subject of anger include: Proverbs 15:1,18; Proverbs 19:11; Proverbs 22:24-25; Proverbs 25:21-22; Proverbs 29:20,22; Philippians 2:3-4; Romans 8:6; 12:19-21; and Colossians 3:8.

Let's close out this chapter looking at the invitational hymn entitled "Turn Your Eyes upon Jesus." This song expresses the way in which we can overcome anger — by turning our eyes from self and struggles to the selfish Savior.

O soul, are you weary and troubled?
No light in the darkness you see?
There's light for a look at the Savior,
And life more abundant and free!

Turn your eyes upon Jesus,
Look full in His wonderful face,
And the things of earth will grow strangely dim,
In the light of His glory and grace.

Chapter 6

OVERCOMING LONELINESS

The world has a greater population now more than ever, yet loneliness seems to persist like never before. Someone can live in the largest city, have a big family, be involved in a thriving ministry, and have people all around them while still feeling lonely. Loneliness isn't something that's new. Check out a few people in the Bible that were in the crosshairs of loneliness:

1. David was anointed by God to be the next king, but soon he was being chased by a mad king and forced to live in a cave. He had to leave his family, friends, and comforts because of King Saul's jealousy. David loved God, yet had to live in isolation. Talk about being lonely!

2. Joseph had a dream that he would be a great leader, yet he was sold into slavery by his own brothers. He was mistreated as a slave and his father thought he was dead. Talk about being lonely!

3. Daniel was one of the Hebrew children stolen from his homeland to grow up under the wicked king Nebuchadnezzar. He went from being liked by the authorities to being thrown into a lion's den. Talk about being lonely!

4. Moses was raised as the grandson of Pharaoh. He had the best education, unlimited authority, plenty of money, and pretty much anything he desired. Yet he was exiled to the desert and was soon overlooking livestock. After forty years of being alone in the desert, he led God's people out of Egypt, but then the same people he helped complained and criticized him. Even his siblings turned on him. Talk about being lonely!

5. The Apostle Paul was saved and his life totally changed. His greatest desire was to preach Christ, yet he was rejected by many Christians, run out of town frequently, beaten, stoned, shipwrecked, and hated. Talk about being lonely!

6. The well-known prophet Elijah saw God's miraculous hand manifested in Israel. God sent fire from Heaven when Elijah asked. Israel was turning to God and the enemies of God were defeated. Even so, Elijah ran to a cave to escape everyone. When God asked Elijah what he was doing in the cave, he replied, "I, even I only, am left; and they seek my life, to take it away" (I Kings 19:9-10). He was believing a lie! Elijah was not alone, he just felt like he was. And this same feeling is still happening to many people today. It's not true, but many believe they're alone, that no one cares, that no one understands, and that God has forsaken them.

Much of the loneliness is not a physical problem; it's a false perception of reality. Let's turn the light on loneliness and discover the truth of the matter. Below are some ways we can overcome the loneliness in our lives.

Draw closer.

Let your loneliness drive you to a deeper relationship with God. Loneliness is a test that finds out from where it is that you draw your strength and hope. God longs for His children to get to know Him better. Through prayer, through the Bible, and through crying out to Him, you can use that scary silence and loneliness to draw near to your Creator. The positive side of loneliness is that there are no distractions stopping you from drawing closer and knowing more intimately the One who made and loves you. Praying to God allows you to know someone else is carrying the load with you - God! Singing to God changes your mood, uplifts your spirit, and expresses truths flowing from your heart to God's ears. Quoting or reflecting on God's Word will get your heart and mind out of darkness and into light. Loneliness doesn't have to be the end for you. Allow it to push you closer and into a deeper relationship with God.

Reach out.

A cure for loneliness is to reach out and serve others. I do believe staying busy is good, (after all, an idle mind is the devil's workshop), but reaching out to others is more than just staying busy. Reaching out to others will allow you to forget about your needs and start focusing on the needs and lives of others. If you were to go down to the hospital, local rescue mission, soup kitchen, public school, or any number of needy areas, you would soon find out that there are people with much bigger problems than that of your own. Listen to this saying by Denis E. Waitley: "I had the blues because I had no shoes until upon the street, I met a man who had no feet."

Learn the lost art of hospitality.

Hospitality has to do with receiving or entertaining guests, strangers, or visitors. Since loneliness is a state of mind that pushes people to recluse, hospitality is probably never on a lonely person's radar. Yet God saw fit to tell all Christians to be "given to hospitality" (Romans 12:13). There are many ways to show hospitality, whether opening your house, using your vehicle to help, baking something for others, giving words of encouragement, or simply giving a helping hand where needed. It doesn't matter how you show hospitality, the point is that God wants every one of His children to do it. But God takes a step further by saying He wants His children not only to be hospitable, but to also do it "without grudging" (1 Peter 4:9). In other words, don't just be hospitable, but do it with the right heart attitude. In fact, God says "be not forgetful to entertain (show hospitality to) strangers" (Hebrews 13:2). So why does hospitality even matter, outside of the fact that God commands us to do it? Because it's always better to give than to receive (Acts 20:35). It does something for your own heart when you break free from dwelling on yourself and begin receiving, helping, and entertaining others. As you set aside the concern for yourself and focus on serving others, the stone of loneliness is broken, your mood changes, others are helped, and you are following your Heavenly Father's instructions. The lost art of hospitality is a great solution to overcome loneliness!

Manage your time better.

Getting out of the house, out of bed, and busy fulfilling both your responsibilities as well as your goals will help shake much of the loneliness. It's not that business solves all loneliness, but the less time one has to be alone and think on their own struggles is for the better. The devil whispers in the ears of many Christians that no one loves them, they don't matter, and it's not worth it. Not having the luxury of staying home, being alone, or having too much free time will minimize much of the loneliness. Pull out a piece of paper, write down every day of the week, and start plugging in your job hours, your responsibilities, and your goals. Maybe there's yard work that needs done, a neighbor that needs helped, a project you've always wanted to get to, or some personal reading and studying. Start managing your time better and you might just smother out the loneliness from your life.

Let's close out this chapter meditating on the good old hymn entitled "What a Friend We Have in Jesus." The song will do you good to think upon, pray, and even sing out to God.

Are we weak and heavy-laden,

Cumbered with a load of care?

Precious Savior, still our refuge—

Take it to the Lord in prayer.

Do thy friends despise, forsake thee?

Take it to the Lord in prayer!

In His arms He'll take and shield thee,

Thou wilt find a solace there.

Chapter 7

OVERCOMING PRIDE

Everyone struggles with pride to some degree. To deny you don't struggle with pride is probably an indicator that pride is a bigger problem than you originally imagined. The manifestations of pride are usually different for every person. Some people are loud and others very quiet. Pride has been around since before mankind. It can flare up at any stage of life, and has taken down many good Christians. Pride causes people to not know the Lord (Psalm 10:4) and Christians to not grow in the Lord. Pride is an abomination to God (Proverbs 6:16-17; 16:5) and always brings shame to whoever possesses it (Proverbs 11:2). It was pride that caused Lucifer, the devil, to fall (Isaiah 14:12-15), as well as many great leaders (Nebuchadnezzar, Herod, and King Saul to name a few). Pride is a sickness that is not easily detected by others, but is certainly fatal to the beholder. So instead of discussing our battle with pride, let's jump right in and discuss some proven Biblical ways to overcome this nasty problem.

Don't think so highly of yourself.

The intention is not to get you to beat yourself up, or to walk around with false humility, but to be honest with yourself. Listen to what the apostle Paul advises the Christians in Rome: "For I say, through the grace given unto me, to every man that is among you, not to think of himself more highly than he ought to think; but to think soberly, according as God hath dealt to every man the measure of faith" (Romans 12:3).

Have you ever considered where humans came from? According to the Bible, in Genesis 2:7, God made mankind out of the dust of the ground. How much is dirt worth? When I was a missionary in Argentina, an evangelist friend told me that the chemicals in the human body amounted up to about 7 pesos (equivalence of $2.50 at that time). This isn't to belittle your worth as a person, but to cause a reality check. Too many times we walk around like a peacock thinking we're all that and a bag of chips, when in reality, we probably think way too highly of ourselves.

It might be that God has gifted you with evident talents, financial security, or strong intelligence, but God warns you about thinking too highly of yourself. The wise king Solomon said, "Let another man praise thee, and not thine own mouth; a stranger, and not thine own lips." (Proverbs 27:1-2). Self-proclaimed greatness is not really greatness. Don't forget that it's God who gave you what you have, and it's God who can take from you what He has given to you. Pride wants you to think that you're the greatest, so be cautious of thinking too highly of yourself.

Don't take the credit for success.

My pastor used to tell me about the "grace sandwich." You have to work harder than almost anyone, but in the end the success is because of God. I thought the advice was genius, but this concept was not original with him, it comes straight from the Bible. Listen to the Bible's way of saying it: "But by the grace of God I am what I am: and his grace which was bestowed upon me was not in vain; but I laboured more abundantly than they all: yet not I, but the grace of God which was with me." (1 Corinthians 15:10). To see children raised for Jesus, a ministry built, and people trained to lead in ministry is all by the grace of God, plus a lot of hard work. God's grace and man's efforts do not contradict each other, they complement each other. Shame on the man who sits back expecting God to work but doesn't give it his all. But even greater shame to take the credit when it's time to give away the credit. You'd better work hard, but when the credit ribbons are being passed out, don't forget Who gave you the success!

I heard a joke about a woodpecker who was pecking a telephone pole. He was working hard to find some bugs even though the rain was falling heavily. Out of seemingly nowhere, a lightning bolt hit the telephone pole, and it exploded. The woodpecker fell to the ground but quickly jumped back up to look at the pole. He stood to his feet, pushed out his chest, and said, "Look at the explosion I just made!" When something wonderful is accomplished, we should remember that, although we were busy at our job, it was God who caused the explosion of success.

God teaches us to give honor to whom honor is due (Romans 13:7). No one arrived at where they are alone. Parents, teachers, friends, coworkers, pastors, and mentors were a few of the people God used in your life to get you where you are. Don't forget that. In fact, when was the last time you wrote one of them a letter thanking them for the role they played in your life? Don't only give honor to whom honor is due, but give credit to whom credit is due. Pride tells you that you made it to this point by yourself, but be honest and give credit to those who helped you arrive where God has placed you.

Avoid entitlement.

Too many people in our world think and act as if they are entitled. They think no one can correct them, improve on their work, or get anything done without them. The entitled attitude has caused everyone to get a trophy, no one to be fired from a job, and minimum wage and benefits to continue improving whether someone does their job or not. "Entitlement" is a fancy word for "pride." Entitled people expect to be thanked, respected, consulted, and appreciated. Entitled people get their feelings hurt easily, not because they were really mistreated, but because their expectations of how they should be treated were more than what is considered reasonable.

My pastor frequently says that many Christians want to be considered a servant until they are treated like one. Here are a few gut-wrenching questions to ask yourself: How do you handle being corrected? How would you respond if a list of names was given for doing something and your name was left out? What if no one thanked you? What if you were told to do something, in an impolite manner, by someone who does not have a position over you? The questions above may seem mean, but they reveal how entitled you feel. Pride is reactionary and jumps up way too fast, which is not a good thing. God says that He resists the proud but gives more grace to the humble (James 4:6; Proverbs 3:34; 1 Peter 5:5).

Try some new vocabulary words.

There are several words or phrases that a prideful person usually avoids: “Thank you,” “I’m sorry,” and, “I messed up.” It’s not a weak person who admits when they are wrong, it’s a wise person. In fact, according to Proverbs 13:10, “Only by pride cometh contention.” The arguments all start or become stronger because of pride. If you want to avoid or stop a fight, then get rid of the pride. If you want to get rid of the pride, then change your vocabulary. It won’t kill you to say you’re sorry, to admit you did wrong, to accept the idea from someone else, or to thank them for what they’ve done. Changing your vocabulary will not only rid you of much pride, it will probably gain you many friends.

I heard the story of a mother who was pushing her child in a cart as she was grocery shopping. The manager happened to be walking by and noticed the kid sitting still in the cart. The manager picked up one of the best-looking apples he could find, cleaned it off with a towel, and smilingly gave it to the child. The mother looked at her child and said, "What do you tell the man for giving you an apple?" The kid looked at his apple, then to the manager, and said, "Peel it!" The kid apparently never learned gratitude. And this is exactly how pride thinks and speaks. Instead of using words to show gratitude, pride creeps up and demands more. Make sure your words don't give any hint of pride. Fix the thoughts in your heart and you won't have to worry about the words that come out of your mouth.

Choose humility.

Humility is often confused with thinking extremely poor of oneself or of life in general. That's not humility at all! A better explanation was given by author Ken Blanchard when he said, "Humility isn't thinking less of yourself, it's thinking of yourself less." In fact, God has respect for the humble (Psalm 138:6) whereas the proud in heart is an abomination to Him (Proverbs 16:5). You can humble yourself or let God humble you. The good news is that you can choose. Humbling yourself would be putting others first, not thinking you're the greatest, and acknowledging God and others instead of thinking you accomplished something alone. If you continue in pride, God says you will be humbled (Matthew 23:12). It's easier to humble yourself than be humbled by God, or even humbled by others. Choose humility!

Think about a tool such as a hammer boasting itself about how amazing it is. Without the person to use the tool, the tool is useless. And that was the exact lesson God gave Isaiah about the boasting of Israel (Isaiah 10:15). God may have made you smart, strong, or given you money and abilities, but your only boasting should be that you know the Lord (Jeremiah 9:23-24). Talk about how good God is, not how good you are. Praise is lifting up another while pride is lifting up yourself. Praise and lift up Christ, not yourself! Choose humility!

Let's close out this chapter by meditating on the old hymn entitled "I Need Thee Every Hour." The words to the song take the focus off of oneself and places it on Christ, the One that we truly need.

I need Thee every hour, most gracious Lord;
No tender voice like Thine can peace afford.

I need Thee, oh, I need Thee;
Every hour I need Thee;
Oh, bless me now, my Savior,
I come to Thee.

Chapter 8

OVERCOMING LAZINESS

Sadly, we all have a laziness streak. Some overcome it and some give into it, but it exists within everyone. God says that we should work for the night is coming (John 9:4); we are to occupy until He comes (Luke 19:13); we are not to grow weary in well doing (Galatians 6:9); and we are to show our faith by our works (James 2:18). As God's children, we must learn to kick the laziness out of our lives before it steals the joy and blessings God has in store for us. We cannot merely blame laziness on a personality type. Whether introvert or extrovert, driven or laid back, shy or outgoing, everyone can and must learn to overcome laziness. Let's do a little thinking and use the following stepping stones to get us across the river of laziness.

Place routines in your life.

In January 2004, my wife and I arrived the country of Argentina to serve as missionaries. Our desire was to start churches and prepare leaders to take over those churches. The desires were strong, but that's all they were: desires. Within two weeks of arriving in Argentina, we found our house and moved in. We started looking for a place to start our first church, but we were working from scratch. I decided I would begin leaving my house every morning at 8:00 a.m. and stay out until around 4:00 p.m. At first, I had no contacts, no church building, and no real job structure, but I knew I had to place the routine of leaving my house and working. Over time, contacts were made, the first church was started, I began teaching others the Bible, and the church and ministry began to grow. Later, the first church was on its feet, the second was started, the Bible college was going strong, and my responsibilities were laid out more clearly. I knew that before the ministries grew, I had to start with the basics by placing routines in my own life. And this same principle has to apply to each one of us in every stage of life. We must create routines in which we can start working. Your routines might simply be to wake up at a certain hour, to talk to a certain number of people, to read at a certain time, or to set aside a certain day or timeframe to work on what you want to accomplish. When you place routines in your life by blocking off chunks of time, you are on your way to accomplishing more.

Make yourself accountable.

Whether you write down your goals or announce it to friends, you have to make yourself accountable. For example, if you want to start reading your Bible every day, then make yourself accountable by writing down and sharing what you read with a friend. Whatever your goal or responsibility is, let someone else know you want them to ask you and keep you accountable. If you know someone is going to ask you where you were, what you were doing, or why you haven't finished something, you'll be more likely to shake off the laziness and do it.

Write a list of motives.

Get out a piece of paper. Make yourself a list of items that will motivate you to get up and do what needs to be done. Maybe it's a person you want to please, the feelings or rewards you will have when you finish the task, or simply knowing you are one step closer to the goal. Knowing you have a reason to do something might be just what you need to overcome that lazy bone. According to 1 Corinthians 15:58, what we do for the Lord is not in vain (useless or pointless). Later, in Hebrews 6:10, it says, "For God is not unrighteous to forget your work and labour of love." God doesn't forget or leave His children rewardless — now that's a motive that encourages and keeps a Christian moving! You must find motives for your own life. Your motive might be knowing that what you do helps your spouse, your children, your parents, or your friends. Your motive might be that what you do brings satisfaction, completion to a project, or fulfills a need. Your motive might be knowing you want to please God (2 Timothy 2:4) or you want to glorify God (1 Corinthians 10:31). Whatever the motive is, state it clearly in your mind or on paper, and keep it in front of you. Having motives might be exactly what you need to give you purpose and free yourself from laziness.

Begin new disciplines and stick with them.

Laziness usually goes hand in hand with being unorganized and undisciplined. You will not get far in life without discipline. You need discipline to get up, to work, to make progress in any area, and to fulfill your roles and responsibilities. Neglecting discipline in your life is like trying to breathe under water — you have a short amount of time before life ends. The absence of discipline causes marriages and families to be wounded, jobs to be terminated, and much ground to be lost. Write down what disciplines are essential for your life, and be consistent to put them into practice. Ask others to help you know what areas you need to place discipline in your life, and take it seriously. Whether you put alarms on your phones, sticky notes on your mirrors, or enlist friends to remind you what you need to be doing, take the serious and drastic step of putting discipline in your life. Just as a flower needs the sun to survive and thrive, you need discipline in your life to survive and thrive. Do you really want to kick the laziness out of your life? Discipline will be your guard dog to protect you.

Let's close out this chapter meditating on the old hymn entitled "Work, for the Night Is Coming." The words to the song are a kick in the pants to not only remind us to work for our Lord, but to give us a motivation of why to work for our Lord.

Work, for the night is coming,
Work through the morning hours;
Work while the dew is sparkling,
Work 'mid springing flow'rs.
Work when the day grows brighter,
Work in the glowing sun;
Work, for the night is coming,
When man's work is done.
Work, for the night is coming,
Under the sunset skies;
While their bright tints are glowing,
Work, for daylight flies.
Work till the last beam fadeth,
Fadeth to shine no more;
Work, while the night is dark'ning,
When man's work is o'er.

Chapter 9

OVERCOMING STAGNATION

When I was growing up, our house was close to the Little Blue River. We enjoyed it for some fishing, canoeing, and goofing around. Because the river had many curves, years before, portions of the river were cut off so the river would flow in a straighter path. One of these cut-off portions of the river was on my parents' property was. Growing up, we called it "the slew." We used to go down to the slew to catch frogs, shoot snapping turtles, and just have fun. Since the slew didn't have water entering or exiting, the water was stagnant, stunk horribly, and had very little life other than what was left over from when it was originally cut off. Almost every time we went down to look for frogs, snakes, and turtles, we would inevitably slip into the muddy water. The smell was very peculiar because of the stagnant water. As we would walk back towards the house, we would have to take off our shoes and socks, and even then the bad odor stayed on us. Stagnation and a horrible stench were signs of little to no life.

Life has a way of wearing us down, sucking the joy out of our marriage, friendships, activities, and spiritual walk. It's easy and almost inevitable to become stagnant at different times. But we must not forget that stagnation both stinks and offers little to no life.

God wants His children to be full of life and to continue growing, yet stagnation swallows up life and thrives on rottenness. God even commands His children to grow (1 Corinthians 15:58, 2 Peter 3:18). What areas do you need to grow in? Make a list of the roles and responsibilities God has given you. Are you a parent? A spouse? A spiritual leader? A student? Be honest with yourself examine, and admit if you're growing in the roles and responsibilities God has given you. Now take that list, and begin to write down how you can grow in each area. Whether it's to take your spouse on a date, read a book for your personal growth, write a letter of gratitude to those under or over you, or spend some time with someone, you have to determine how you are going to grow in the roles and responsibilities God has given you. Stagnation is not a place anyone should live, it's a choice. So choose to break free from the stagnation and begin to grow and flourish once again!

In 2 Timothy 1:6, Paul told Timothy that God was the One who placed the fire inside of him, but it was Timothy's responsibility to keep it hot. Just as a fire goes out without wood, so the fire in one's heart will go out if it's not fed. Every Christian has the responsibility to keep his fire (desire, zeal, or passion for God) stoked so it doesn't go out. The storms of life are certain for every individual, but we cannot let the storms quench our love and fire for God. Keep your passion alive by daily reading the Bible, being faithful to church, sharing your faith, reading missionary biographies, and associating with those who are committed and happily serving God. God put a desire inside of you, but it's your responsibility to keep that fire hot.

I remember as a teenager that our church held a watch night service every year. We would start service around 9:00 p.m. and go until midnight, welcoming in the new year. There would be food, preaching by multiple men, singing, and a couple of Christian films shown. One of the films that greatly impacted me was called Sheffey. It was the story of Robert S. Sheffey, a 19th-century circuit-riding preacher that had a deep-rooted relationship with God. He kept a lamb skin on his horse, and he would lay it on the ground to pray. God used this in my life, and throughout my high school years I would put a deer hide in my backpack and go to the woods to pray. I remember the love, desire, and passion I had to go alone and talk to God. It burned inside of me to know more intimately the God who saved me. I wanted to wholeheartedly seek and serve Him.

I wish I could stop my story there, ending on a high note. But as time went by, life became more fast-paced, responsibilities grew, and opportunities abounded. I cringe to say it, but the Lord received the short end of the stick. No longer did I have time to walk into the woods and get alone with God. Those were the moments of my deep-rooted relationship and walk with God. My strength today was coming from the moments back then. But I must not become stagnant. I cannot depend only on the past to continue in the present and future. How can I get back that love and zeal from before so my life does not become a cold, stagnated one?

Revelation 2-3 speaks about the letters to the seven churches. Chapter 2 verses 1-5 is directed to the church of Ephesus. The church was first commended for their love and good works, but quickly God confronted them about their problem of losing their first love. God gave them the steps to return back to that love and zeal they once possessed. And the same steps God gave Ephesus are both applicable and helpful today for those who have become stagnant in their lives.

Remember.

Do you remember the original desire you had? If we discuss the love and desire for God, you might remember the excitement of going to church, the thrill of sharing your faith, the joy of singing songs of praise, or the peace of God working in your life. If we discuss the love and desire of marriage, you might remember how you used to love to get home to see your spouse, go out on a date, take walks, or just spend time together. Whatever area you have become stagnant in, you must remember how it used to be before so you can work your way back.

Repent.

Once you remember, you must find out what stole your heart, how you arrived to the place of stagnation, and then repent. Ask forgiveness from God and anyone else that is involved. This is more than mere words that fall from your lips. It must be a true understanding and change of direction from within yourself.

Redo.

Now that you remember what caused you to arrive to this place of stagnation and repented of it, it's time to start walking the path back to joyfulness. What habits did you practice that grew your love for God? Let's say we're discussing marriage. Maybe the original acts you did were to intentionally think about your spouse throughout the day, buy little gifts, use kind words, or deliberately spend time together. It's time to redo what you originally did if you want to break free of a stagnate relationship. Make your list and begin to consistently work on it.

Let's close out this chapter meditating on the old hymn entitled "I Gave My Life for Thee." The song is a reflective song asking "What have you given for me?" Although salvation is not merited by anything we can do, the Christian service should be filled with good works done for our Savior born from a heart of gratitude. So read the words and ask yourself what you are doing for Him after all He has done for you. This truth should shake us from the state of stagnation to a life sold out and committed fully to Christ!

I gave My life for thee,
My precious blood I shed,
That thou might ransomed be,
And raised up from the dead;

I gave, I gave My life for thee,
What hast thou giv'n for Me?
I gave, I gave My life for thee,
What hast thou giv'n for Me?
I suffered much for thee,
More than thy tongue can tell,
Of bitt'rest agony,
To rescue thee from hell;
I've borne, I've borne it all for thee,
What hast thou borne for Me?
I've borne, I've borne it all for thee,
What hast thou borne for Me?

Chapter 10

OVERCOMING BAD HABITS

Bad habits can be either destructive or distractive. Destructive habits are such things as drinking, drugs, or unfaithfulness. Distractive habits could be talking bad of others, procrastination, laziness, lying, or insincerity. It's pretty obvious to everyone why one should avoid destructive habits, but distractive habits fly under the radar and, in the long run, end up doing much damage. But whether the habits are sinfully destructive, or simply distractive, bad habits are hard to break. Once something is formed in your mind as normal behavior in your life, it is very difficult to change. But a child of God is an overcomer, and overcoming is not just possible but certain! So let's discuss how to kick those bad habits out of your life.

The reflective method:

1. Is the habit constructive or destructive? Don't just assume since a habit is not destructive that it is automatically constructive. Is

what you're going to do beneficial, useful, and advantageous? (1 Corinthians 6:12, 10:23)

2. Does the habit make you stronger or weaker? Does it weaken or strengthen the roles and responsibilities (as a spouse, a parent, a friend, a worker, or a Christian) that God has given you?

3. Does the habit enslave you or free you? If the habit begins to control you negatively, maybe it's time to break free of it.

4. Does the habit lift God up or put God down? Is your habit pointing others to the Lord or deflecting them from the Lord?

You must decide who is going to be the master of your life. As a Christian, you should be controlled by the Holy Spirit, not by the bad habits that have latched on to your life. If you're going to be addicted to something, take the advice from 1 Corinthians 16:15 and be addicted to God and His service.

The replacement method:

Throughout the Bible there is a principle that is both powerful and practical. This principle, found in Romans 13:12-14, Ephesians 4:22-25, Colossians 3:8-14, James 1:21, and 1 Peter 2:1-2, commands a Christian to cast off certain habits and put on other habits. Whether an attitude or action, it must be replaced with God's solution, or it will linger. For example, bitterness must be replaced with forgiveness. Hatred must be replaced with love. Laziness must be replaced with discipline. Stealing must be replaced with honest work. Bad influence must be replaced with good influence. Pride must be replaced with humility. Fear must be replaced with faith. Negativity must be replaced with Biblical thinking. You must first pinpoint the bad habit in your life, and then replace it with the correct habit. The best way to apply the replacement method is to know God's Word and follow God's wisdom. Proverbs is a great place to start reading and learning more about the practical truths God wants to teach you in your everyday life.

Let's close out this chapter meditating on the old hymn entitled "I Surrender All." The words should be a prayer from the heart of every child of God. Surrendering bad habits or obstacles should be the natural desire of God's children.

All to Jesus I surrender,
All to Him I freely give;
I will ever love and trust Him,
In His presence daily live.

I surrender all,
I surrender all;
All to Thee, my blessed Savior,
I surrender all.
All to Jesus I surrender,
Humbly at His feet I bow;
Worldly pleasures all forsaken,
Take me, Jesus, take me now.

I surrender all,

I surrender all;

All to Thee, my blessed Savior,

I surrender all.

Chapter 11

OVERCOMING VICTIMHOOD

Although there are many horrible evils in our world, it has become acceptable and even popular to take on the attitude of being a victim. The problem with being a victim is that many people become immobile or paralyzed, not believing they can ever overcome what has happened to them. God's children are victors, not victims! You can overcome what has happened to you. You do not have to stay defeated or allow a bad event or hurtful memory to bind you. Here are a few truths to help you as you strive to overcome the bad things that happened to you in your life.

You're not alone.

John 16:33 says that in this world you will have tribulation. That doesn't seem like good news until you come to the end of the verse, where our Lord says we can be of good cheer because He has overcome the world. When God's Word is our source of information and instruction, it changes the way we look at things. We were never promised we would be happy, healthy, and wealthy. That's like the lie the devil told Eve, saying God didn't really want her to be happy. If God's plan is for you to be happy, then there's nothing wrong with stealing money to have more, leaving your spouse because you like someone else, or any number of other excuses for selfish pleasures. God gives us joys, but God also allows trials. Don't buy into the idea that if you have problems, God doesn't love you.

Does it anchor or fuel you?

Everyone must decide if they're going to allow their past, their problems, or their struggles to be an anchor that holds them down or a fuel that thrusts them forward. What has driven some to depression, bitterness, or excuses to why they cannot continue has been allowed of others to become the motivation that pushes them forward to prosper. Yes, it's true that some people have been given opportunities and open doors have been handed to them, but that doesn't mean it's impossible for you. You can decide to put in double the effort, pray, and work towards the goal. With determination and hard work, it is possible to catch up and even pass the "privileged" person. Some of the greatest leaders of our time have risen from poverty, abuse, a bad home life, or little education. What was the perfect excuse for some to be immobile has been the exact reason others have become better. You must decide to let God use your past or current circumstances to do more, not do less.

Accept your past and thank God.

Hating your past, blaming others, or harboring bitterness, will never let you properly move forward in life. Whether your past is that of abuse, mistreatment, poverty, or any sort of bad experiences, you must learn to accept it. Blaming God or others will not change your past, it will only make you feel worse. Fighting or dwelling on your difficulties will not free you, but rather enslave you to a deeper self-pity.

Read the attitude of David in Psalms 16:5-6: "The Lord is the portion of mine inheritance and of my cup: thou maintainest my lot. The lines are fallen unto me in pleasant places; yea, I have a goodly heritage." He says that what God had given him was not just good, it was an admirable portion or possession. But even more amazing is that he did not write this when he was living in the palace eating grapes and lying in a king-sized bed. He wrote this when he was living in a cave, sleeping on the ground without his family, and being mistreated by his own countrymen. He wrote this when he was on the run from a mad and jealous king who wanted to kill him. It was at this moment, when others would've been crying in bitterness towards God for such a horrible life, that David said, "thank you" to God. He didn't just accept what God had given him, he actually thanked God for it.

Theoretically, everyone knows you are to give thanks in everything (1 Thessalonians 5:18) and be joyful even in trials (James 1:3), but it's easier to know than it is to put it into practice. If God has allowed or is allowing you to go through hard times, maybe He wants to use it so you can help others. Accept what God has placed in your life, thank Him, and let Him use it for His glory.

Learn from the prodigal's brother.

You remember the story of the prodigal son in Luke 15? The story consists of two brothers and a loving father. The younger brother was egotistical and impatient, wanting his inheritance immediately instead of waiting until later in life. I'm sure his dad hurt badly as he gave the selfish son his future inheritance. The son then went and spent all he had living a wasted and empty life. Finally, he ran out of money, and his lovers, friends, and fans all abandoned him, forcing him to eat slop with the pigs. The son recognized that he made a grave mistake, decided to swallow his pride, and headed back home. He hoped his dad would have pity on him. It proved true. The loving father received him with open arms and threw a giant party for his wayward son who returned home. But as his dad was rejoicing that his son had come home, the older brother became livid. Why would his dad kill the fatted calf and throw a party for the younger brother who had wasted all that he had in the first place? The older brother was right. He was the one who had stayed to help and had been faithful and loyal, yet the bratty, younger brother was the one who received the party. It was just unfair!

I find it a little odd the Bible concludes the story there. It doesn't appear the dad reprimands the younger, egotistical and sinful brother. He just tells the older brother to be happy the younger brother is back home. It seems very unfair! The older brother is the victim. He was faithful, loyal, honest, and true to his dad, but he gets no party. But there are some lessons in here for everyone:

- God doesn't want us to focus on others, but to focus on Him. We are not everyone else's judge, we must continue doing right ourselves.

- God wants us to be happy for others. If we are going to look at others, we are to be happy for them, not jealous or envious of them.

- God expects us to do right no matter what others do. Whether others walk away, offend us, mistreat us, curse God, or curse us, we are still supposed to do right.

It seems unfair that the younger brother was rebellious, wasted funds, and was unappreciative to his dad, yet he still got the party. The older brother probably felt like the victim here and could've started his own support group, but neither his dad nor Scripture gave room for it. God's teaching isn't based on your feelings, and God's principles stand firm in spite of your feelings. The victim mentality will lead you to follow feelings, but God wants you to walk by faith.

Where's your focus?

The victim mentality is a sure and quick way to gain attention. Many books, quotes, songs, and groups seem to center around being victimized. Although there certainly are people who have been hurt, the victim mentality thrives on being self-focused. God's Word and

God's way places the focus on Christ, not on man's hardships and feelings. This is not to say that God doesn't care about feelings, but that God wants His children to be focused on Him more than on their feelings. God tells His followers to deny themselves (Mark 8:34), to not think it strange to go through trials (1 Peter 4:12), to rejoice in persecution (Matthew 5:10-12), and to realize that offenses will come (Matthew 18:7). Difficulties, trials, and hard times are not abnormal for a believer, it's part of life. We are told that if we faint in the day of adversity, our strength is small (Proverbs 24:10). If you are focused on yourself, there will be plenty of opportunities to become offended. If you are focused on God and His Word, you can have peace and not be offended (Psalm 119:165). Your focus will determine your feeling. Being a victim is rooted in focusing on self while being a victor is rooted in being focused on Christ!

Let's close out this chapter meditating on the true old hymn entitled "I Shall Not Be Moved." The words are powerful and will help you avoid the victim mentality. There are plenty of things in this world that will knock you down and cause you to want to quit, but this song teaches us to stay rooted in the eternal Christ and not be uprooted by the storms of life.

Though all hell assail me, I shall not be moved.
Jesus will not fail me, I shall not be moved.
Just like a tree that's planted by the waters,
I shall not be moved.
Though the tempest rages, I shall not be moved.
On the Rock of Ages, I shall not be moved.
Just like a tree that's planted by the waters.
I shall not be moved.

Chapter 12

OVERCOMING DOUBT

Kids believe almost anything. You can tell a child that pigs fly, superman is real, you once visited the moon, or some cows give chocolate milk, and they're almost certain to believe you. But when adulthood approaches, most people become very skeptical. The good side of not believing everything is that you're not so easily taken advantage of, but the bad side of doubting is that it can kick faith out of the equation.

Stick with faith, not feelings.

Feelings come and go, but a child of God must learn to believe God no matter how they feel. You may feel like you're not saved, like God doesn't love you, or like something is impossible, but don't throw faith out the window just because of your feelings. Remember that whatever God says, it is always true, regardless of how you act or feel. Romans 3:4 says to let God be true, but every man a liar. In other words, man's lack of belief doesn't change God's existence or promises. So no matter how you feel, make sure you stick with the truth.

Is there a reason you're doubting?

For a couple of years in my youth, I doubted if I was truly saved. I thought maybe I didn't say the prayer exactly right, or maybe I didn't have the right understanding or attitude when I prayed. I was full of doubt, and I wrestled with that doubt for years. When I was a senior in high school, I remember talking to a man that helped me tremendously. I told the man that I wasn't sure if I was saved and I wanted to pray again just in case. The man asked me why I thought God was a liar. "Whoa," I said to the man, "I never said that." He looked at me and said, "No, but you sure act like it." He showed me that God had promised eternal, everlasting life, and that God always fulfills His promises. And he finished by saying, "Either God's a liar, or you're not believing what He said." Well, God doesn't lie, so the fault lies with me.

So why do we doubt? Many times someone doubts because of a problem within their own life. Let's continue with the thought of doubting one's salvation. One might doubt because they legitimately do not know what God's Word teaches (lack of knowledge). Another might doubt because they are not reading God's Word (lack of discipline). Yet another might doubt because they are not living according to God's Word (lack of applying). The problem is not with God, rather with the individual. And this principle can be applied to almost any area of life. The devil, who is the author of confusion, would love to trip you up and make you doubt.

Doubting makes you miserable.

Whether you doubt someone's love for you, if something could be possible, or if you are capable, doubting makes you miserable. Relationships are built on trust and destroyed with doubt. Doubt will force you to give up your dreams or any attempts to progress. Doubting doesn't change reality, but many will never see what could happen because of their doubt. Doubt causes fear, and when fear is present God's love is absent (1 John 4:18). God wants his children to believe Him, but doubt causes His children to question or quit on Him. God wants His children to ask Him for things, but He says to ask believing (Matthew 21:21-22). Ask for wisdom (James 1:5), but don't ask in disbelief (James 1:6). Doubting will quiet you from asking, blind you from seeing what could happen, stop you from attempting, and make you feel miserable all along the way.

Doubting handicaps God's work.

Throughout the life of Christ, it is said multiple times that he did not do many mighty works because of their unbelief (Matthew 13:58; Mark 6:5). There may have been more miracles performed if they would've only believed. But that's not just a truth of the past, that's a reality for our lives today. Do you really believe God can provide for you? Do you really believe God will protect you? Do you really believe God wants to use you? God is not limited because of your abilities.

The boy with the five loaves and the two fish saw five thousand men and their families fed. Can you imagine what he told his friends the next day? His bag of food may have been small, but his faith was big, and God did a mighty work! It really doesn't matter how big your lunch bag is if your faith is small. What a shame it is that God would use someone else because you don't have faith! Too many people miss out on the mighty works because they doubt God. Scripture says Jesus could not do many mighty works in Mark 6:5, and the next verse says that He marveled because of their unbelief. What do you think would cause God to marvel (be amazed or astonished) in your life? Would it be your belief or your unbelief? You must not forget that without faith it is impossible to please God (Hebrews 11:6). God is both willing and capable of doing great things in your life. The question is, will you let Him? You can either facilitate God's working in your life by your faith, or you can handicap it by your doubt.

Doubting is not remembering.

One of my favorite books in the Old Testament is the book of Deuteronomy. Jesus quoted from this book more than any other. Deuteronomy is a book that covers the last month before the children of Israel left the desert to enter into the promised land (Deuteronomy 1:3). It is a summary of everything God said through Moses from the book of Exodus through the book of Numbers. It is a repetition, a reminder of what God had already commanded His people. Throughout the book, the words "remember" and "forget" are used quite a bit. God wanted them to remember what they had seen, had heard, had been commanded, and had been promised. God didn't want them to forget how He provided water from a rock, food from birds, protection from enemies, and clarity along the way. God wanted them to know and remember that He was with them. He told them in chapters 11:2-3: "I speak not with your children which have not known, and which have not seen the chastisement of the LORD your God, his greatness, his mighty hand, and his stretched out arm, and his miracles, and his acts, which he did in the midst of Egypt unto Pharaoh the king of Egypt, and unto all his land." God had dealt with them in a special way, and they were to not forget it.

In my life, I have seen God's blessings, provision, protection, leading, and presence. Every child of God could give witness of God's goodness and greatness in their lives. Yet in moments of fear and doubt, we forget all that God has done and promised in our lives. We, as the children of Israel, must not forget what God has done in our past, and has promised for our future. When we doubt, we are not remembering all that God has done. When we remember God's goodness and greatness, we will not doubt.

Be certain of the future.

You can know, as a child of God, that God is not going to abandon you or leave you to fend for yourself. Matthew 6 teaches that we don't have to worry or doubt His care for us. He clothes the flowers and feeds the birds. How much more does He care for you and me as His children. You might not know the details of tomorrow, but you can know the God who will be with you tomorrow. There's no need to fear when Jesus is near. There's no need to doubt God's capability. He's got this. Rest assured that He will take care of you.

Start believing and stop doubting.

The story of how Abraham believed that God was going to give him a son has to be one of the top Biblical stories when it comes to believing God. Romans 4 unfolds the details of this incredible story. Abraham was promised that he would be the father of many nations, but Isaac wasn't born until he was one hundred years old! The Bible says that Abraham "against hope believed in hope" (Romans 4:18), that he "staggered not at the promise of God through unbelief" (Romans 4:20), and that he was "fully persuaded that, what he had promised, he was able also to perform" (Romans 4:21). Think about it, his wife was well past the time of having children, but he knew that God was going to fulfill the promise he was given. In fact, Sarah, Abraham's wife, gave birth, "when she was past age, because she judged him faithful who had promised" (Hebrews 11:11). This seems to be the power couple for trusting God. They trusted God against their circumstances, even when everyone and everything within them would've said it was impossible. They were persuaded that God was going to fulfill what He had promised.

When my wife and I were raising financial support to go to Argentina, we visited many churches to present our goal and ask if they would partner with us. The desire to get to the mission field was clear for me since I was sixteen years old. I couldn't wait to get to the place God had put in my heart, and finally I was married, out of college, and on my way. On the way from one of our meetings, we stopped at a QuickTrip gas station. I swiped my debit card at the pump and it said, "Error." After a couple more attempts, I decided to fill up on gas and then go in to pay afterwards. I knew I had money on the card; the machine was just not reading it correctly.

As I was pumping gas and waiting, a nice truck with a big boat pulled to the pump next to me. Since I was waiting, I walked a few steps over to make small talk with the truck owner. After normal greetings, I gave him a Gospel tract and told him the most important news in the world was written on the back. We made more small talk and then I walked back over to my vehicle, hung up the hose, and went in to pay. I told the attendant what pump number I was at and handed him my debit card. He swiped it and it didn't work. He tried it a couple more times with no luck. He asked if I had another card and I told him I didn't. He put a plastic bag over it and swiped my card one more time for good measure. He apologized and said the card was not working. I was embarrassed, so I walked outside and asked my wife if she had any money. She didn't have any cash with her and asked me if I had the debit card. I told her I did, but it was not working. We both began to get nervous, looking for change underneath the car seats, in pockets, and in her purse. "Great," I thought to myself, "Now I'm stuck in the middle of nowhere with no money." I continued scrounging for change under the front seat when I heard the truck next to us start up his engine. I poked my head out and politely waved, but I was not in the mood to crack more than half a smile. I was abandoned at a gas station and a bit worried.

Then the truck owner waved for me to come over. I didn't really want to talk, but I walked over anyway. He said thanks for the Gospel tract I gave him, and stuck his hand out to shake my hand. As we shook hands, I noticed there was something between his palm and mine. I was dying to know what it was, but I didn't want to act undignified. I placed my hand in my pocket, thanking the man and saying goodbye.

As soon as his big truck pulled away, I quickly reached my hand into my pocket to find out what he had given me. It was a fifty dollar bill! I went inside to pay the attendant and came running back out to tell my wife. The gas costs about eighteen dollars (obviously that was a while back), that left us with thirty-two dollars. We now had enough money to pay for our gas, go buy lunch, and get ice cream! What a day!

We saw God's miraculous hand multiple times as we were both preparing for the mission field and serving Him there. It is always exciting to see God work in my life, but too many times I still doubt Him when life seems difficult. I must remember what God has done in the past, believe His promises, and know that He is going to do great things in the future. God certainly wants to do great things in our lives. As it says in 1 Corinthians 2:9, "Eye hath not seen, nor ear heard, neither have entered into the heart of man, the things which God hath prepared for them that love him." It's time to stop doubting and start believing!

Let's close out this chapter meditating on the old hymn entitled "All the Way My Savior Leads Me." The words shine the bright light on our doubts by saying, "Jesus doeth all things well." He certainly does! And as a result, there is no reason to doubt, and all the reason to trust Him!

All the way my Savior leads me,
What have I to ask beside?
Can I doubt His tender mercy,
Who through life has been my Guide?
Heav'nly peace, divinest comfort,
Here by faith in Him to dwell!
For I know, whate'er befall me,
Jesus doeth all things well;
For I know, whate'er befall me,
Jesus doeth all things well.

Chapter 13

OVERCOMING UNGRATEFULNESS

Although ungratefulness is not a vice that kills someone, many marriages, friendships, and relationships are greatly harmed because of a lack of gratefulness. Words, actions, and gestures may be shown towards someone, but when gratitude is not reciprocated, soon the person feels used, abused, and unappreciated. Ungratefulness is a poor quality that many kids are growing up with, either because they were not taught how to show basic gratitude, or because their parents never learned gratitude in their own lives. It's not enough just to say, "Well, I am grateful even if I didn't say I was." Gratitude that is unexpressed is not gratitude. An ungrateful person is considered an unthankful, unappreciative, and unpleasant person, and no one enjoys being with that kind of person. Whether through words or actions, gratitude must be expressed. According to the Bible, a man that has friends must show himself friendly (Proverbs 18:24). So how can you show or express friendliness and gratitude to keep friends instead of lose them? Let's talk about how we can easily slip into the category of being ungrateful, and how we can overcome that annoying habit.

Gratitude is important!

According to 1 Thessalonians 5:18, God's will for you is to give thanks in everything. No matter the situation you are in, God wants you to be thankful. It is easy to complain and criticize, but it almost seems like strenuous homework to show gratitude. Are you thankful when the car is broken down, when you're feeling sick, and when you have more bills to pay than money to spare? It's easy to show gratitude to God when all seems to be going well, but the test is when life seems to be beating you up. God wants us to come into His presence with thanksgiving (Psalms 95:2; 100:4), sing to Him with thanksgiving (Psalms 147:7), pray with thanksgiving (Colossians 4:2; Philippians 4:6), and abound with thanksgiving (Colossians 2:7). God loves to hear His children praise Him by giving Him thanks. Whether you praise Him through prayer, singing, or telling others about God, don't forget to thank Him. Are you thankful for and to God? Then tell Him! God loves when His children praise Him.

But let us also remember to be thankful to those around us. Too many people forget to say the simple words, "Thank you." Whether someone paid you a compliment, gave you a gift, invited you over, or simply showed a nice gesture, never forget to say, "Thank you." In a day of emails, texts, and social media, the old traditional thank you card is often considered archaic. But a thank you card would do good to both you and the person to whom you write it. Break out the old ball point pen and card. Jot a short letter of thanks to those God has put in your life. Write a list of those you're grateful for: parents, spouse, children, friends, spiritual leaders, coworkers, teachers, or siblings. Now write three or four sentences to each of them expressing your gratitude. Place it in an envelope and mail it or give it to them the next time you see them. Your expression of thanks will make an impact. And when you've long forgotten about the letter, they will still remember.

Why should we be thankful?

When was the last time you realized that everything you have comes from God? According to James 1:17, "Every good gift and every perfect gift is from above, and cometh down from the Father of lights." There's nothing you have that did not come from God. Your position or blessings in life are not merely a result of your abilities. Your health is not simply because you exercise or eat well. Your children are not a result of your being a good parent. All you have that is good is a gift from God. From the air you breathe to the influence you've been given, all of it is a sweet gift of God. The last chapter of the book of Psalms, the longest book in the Bible, contains only six verses yet says the word "praise" thirteen times. God wants His children to praise Him, and God has been so good that we have innumerable reasons to praise Him.

Thankfulness begins in humility.

Being thankful, in my opinion, is rooted in a realization that you are not better than others. Not being thankful comes from a feeling of expectation or entitlement. If they were doing what they should, why should I thank them? So they did or said something nice to me, but it's because I deserved it. If these last two sentences reveal the way you think, you probably think too highly of yourself. God is good to you because that's God's nature, not because you deserve it. And people might be kind to you, but you should never bank on the fact that it's because you deserve it. If you feel you are unworthy of the kindness of others, you will be thankful for every small thing. If you feel you deserve a certain treatment, you will rarely be grateful. Ungratefulness is rooted in pride whereas gratefulness is rooted in humility. Think more of others and less of yourself, and you will be more of a grateful person.

What are some ways to show thankfulness?

Since we've already alluded to some of these, allow me to quickly list a few ways you can show your gratitude to others:

1. Tell them. Next time you see the person you are grateful for, look them in the eyes and use your words to tell them. Whether publicly or privately, they will remember your words well after you say them.

2. Write them. We know the apostle Paul loved those he worked with because he wrote it down so they could read it.

3. Purchase them a gift. This has more to do with the gesture shown, not the amount that was spent. A gift card, chocolates, or something small says a multitude.

4. Pray for them. It might sound cheap or even cliché, but if you genuinely pray for someone, it means you are thinking of them. Paul gave thanks to God as he prayed for those he loved (Ephesians 1:16, Colossians 1:3, 1 Thessalonians 1:2, 2 Thessalonians 2:13).

5. Spend time with them. Spending time with someone is a bold way of saying you love them. Children, a spouse, and family would rather have their loved one's time than their money. Years ago, I heard someone say that you spell love with the letters "T-I-M-E."

Let's close out this chapter meditating on the hymn entitled "Revive Us Again." The song speaks of a personal revival to praise God. All the praise belongs to Him!

We praise Thee, O God!
For the Son of Thy love,
For Jesus Who died,
And is now gone above.

Hallelujah! Thine the glory.

Hallelujah! Amen.
Hallelujah! Thine the glory.
Revive us again.
All glory and praise
To the Lamb that was slain,
Who hath borne all our sins,
And hath cleansed every stain.

Hallelujah! Thine the glory.
Hallelujah! Amen.
Hallelujah! Thine the glory.
Revive us again.

Chapter 14

OVERCOMING DEPRESSION

There are multiple meanings for depression, but here are a few: unhappiness, downheartedness, despondency, discouragement, despair, hopelessness, desolation, and misery. Because of depression, some people withdraw from most human interaction, get on prescribed medication, or want to give up on life. Depression causes people to feel empty and unwanted. Some snap out of it within a short amount of time, and some seem to live in it for a portion of their life. Although there are times to seek medical help, a large portion of depression can be helped by controlling one's attitude, feelings, and emotions. Allow me to give a few ways to help you overcome depressing stages that frequently linger in the shadows of your mind.

Fix your focus.

Money, styles, and almost everything in this world changes regularly. You will never be able to please everyone, be the coolest person, or keep up with the latest trends. If you focus on the wrong things, you will become discouraged and depressed. Many deathbed confessions have revealed a unsatisfied focus. The dying person wishes they would have spent more time with family, thought more of God, and lived more for others. No one should have to come to the end of life before reevaluating their life, so do it now. What are you focusing on? Don't run after something that can never satisfy you, look to Jesus. Don't live for what will not fulfill you. Life is rushing by you. Enjoy what God has given you and where God has placed you. Living for success (materially or ministerially) is a moving target. Learn to be satisfied where God has placed you, with whom God has associated you, and in the position God has given you. Don't focus on your struggles, focus on your blessings. Don't focus on the obstacles, focus on the opportunities. Don't focus on what you don't have, focus on what you do have. Just as a picture is blurry because of bad focus, your life will also be blurry if you don't have the right focus.

Although this is not to sound harsh, much depression can be very egotistical. It's easy to get into a slump because someone didn't treat you right, recognize your work, remember who you are, or thank you for what you've done. The "me-focus" craves attention and gets bent out of shape when forgotten. If you can focus on God and others, it will starve this mentality, and depression will be put to death.

Focus on the job and the responsibilities God has given you. The Bible compares Christians to soldiers, athletes, and farmers, all who must work hard and not quit when times get tough. The soldier endures hardness and stays on mission. The athlete is constantly striving for the win. And the farmer is working both early and late in order to get the desired crop. The end product is not controlled by the individual, but the process that will lead to the product is within our control. You must keep working the process to see the product. Keep fulfilling your job and the responsibilities God has given you, and in God's timing, you will see the fruit of the product. Stay focused and do your part.

Focus on who you are in Christ. If you are a child of God, you are "accepted in the beloved" (Ephesians 1:6). Whether or not others accept, like, or love you, you can know for sure that God accepts, likes, and loves all of His children. I love the response Jesus gave to His disciples after they returned from seeing miracles happen. They returned bragging about what they did and saw. Instead of congratulating them, Jesus told them that their focus should be on the fact that their names were written in Heaven (Luke 10:20). What a lesson for us today! We get so carried away with what we accomplish and lose sight of the most important area of life, that we are God's children. Never lose focus of who you are. Everything else will seem secondary to that fact.

Don't follow your heart.

It seems like an innocent little cliché to say, "follow your heart" when you need to make a decision, but it's not sound advice. According to Jeremiah 17:9, your heart is deceitful above all things. Feelings come and go, so don't follow your heart. Follow something greater than a good feeling, something much firmer, something unchangeable. Follow God and His unchanging Word. God has never led anyone astray, and you will not be the exception. When you need to make a decision, follow God's commands and God's principles. If there's not a specific verse on what you should do, find out if there's a principle in God's Word that will guide you. Keep your heart sensitive to the Lord, but make sure nothing you do is contrary to what God teaches.

Is it something you can control?

Your past and your future are portions of life that cannot be changed or controlled. Many negative feelings and worries are from thoughts that are out of our control. Whether it was something that was said or done to you, or something you said or did to someone else in the past, you must realize that it is in the past. If you can apologize or seek understanding for something, by all means do it. But beating yourself up over something that is out of your control is not worth it. Maybe you have been through a divorce, abuse, or a bad time in the past, but replaying what was said or done back then will not change the past no matter how hard you try. Dale Carnegie said, "All the king's horses and all the king's men can't put the past together again.

So let's remember: Don't try to saw sawdust." Trying to change what is out of your control will cause you to become depressed or continue to live in depression.

Is the problem another person? Maybe something your spouse, neighbor, friend, or parent does is driving you crazy. If you are depressed because of something they've done or said to you, you have two choices: either you need to distance yourself if it is truly toxic, or you need to think differently of that person. Allow me to remind you that you cannot change others, you can only change yourself. Maybe you need to change the way you think or act towards another person, and when your perception is changed, then it will seem the person has changed as well. Romans 12:18 talks about living peaceably with all men, if it's possible, as much as lies within you. There are times that it is not possible, but much could be salvaged if we did everything within ourselves to make it possible. Pray for the person, change the way you speak to them, and be kind to them. It might just be the game changer for the way you feel about the other person. Either way, you do not have to live depressed because of another person. Control what you can and don't try to control what is not within your power.

Nail down the source.

Why are you feeling how you are feeling? Is it a relationship you need to end? Is it an attitude you need to fix within yourself? Is it something you are doing? If you can pinpoint the reason you are depressed, you are on track to overcoming your feelings. God tells us in 2 Corinthians 10:5 that we are to filter all of our thoughts, taking them captive and submitting them to Him. If a thought is not from God, then don't allow that thought to linger. Is it God that's telling you that you're unloved, unwanted, and unworthy? Of course not. If you know the source is not God, then take those thoughts captive to His power. There should be no room for ungodly thoughts. Philippians 4:8 commands us to think only upon that which is true, honest, just, pure, lovely, of good report, or on what has virtue and praise. So, find out the source of your depression, and if it's not from God, uproot those thoughts and throw them in the weed pile to be scorched by the sun.

Let's close out this chapter meditating on the old hymn entitled "I Must Tell Jesus." No one can bear their burdens alone, but thankfully you can tell Jesus, the One who can and will help you!

I must tell Jesus all of my trials,
I cannot bear these burdens alone;
In my distress He kindly will help me,
He ever loves and cares for His own.

I must tell Jesus! I must tell Jesus!
I cannot bear my burdens alone;
I must tell Jesus! I must tell Jesus!
Jesus can help me, Jesus alone.
I must tell Jesus all of my troubles,
He is a kind, compassionate Friend;
If I but ask Him He will deliver,
Make of my troubles quickly an end.

I must tell Jesus! I must tell Jesus!

I cannot bear my burdens alone;

I must tell Jesus! I must tell Jesus!

Jesus can help me, Jesus alone.

Chapter 15

OVERCOMING FAILURE

Between my third and fourth grade years, my family moved, and I entered into a new school. My real love was being outside to hunt, fish, or play sports. Doing homework was not on my radar. I was warned and even disciplined for not doing my schoolwork, but I stood my stubborn ground. It was not a surprise when I failed that year. I was taken to another school district where I attended summer school to try catching up, but I failed there as well. At the start of the next school year, I was taken to yet another school to repeat the fourth grade. Finally, after the third attempt, they let me pass!

Even when I made it to high school, I had difficulty with basic reading. But reading was only one of the many areas in which I struggled. I was too short for the basketball team, rebellious towards authority, and had almost no interest in anything that had to do with academics. Over and over, I seemed to fail. But failures ended up being the greatest thing that could have happened to me. It was through failures that I was challenged to work harder, change my attitude, not quit, and finish the job. God used my dad to teach me much about failure and not giving up. He grew up in poor and difficult circumstances, "But," he would tell me, "anyone can get out of bad conditions if they are willing to work hard enough." His life motivated me to not accept failure, but to work hard and understand that anything can be overcome. Allow me to present some ways that anyone, no matter how bad the situation may seem, can overcome failure.

Learn from your failures.

Failure does not have to be final. In fact, it can be the great instructor you need. When my daughters were very young, we used to warn them to keep their fingers away from light sockets. All my children had been warned several times, but my oldest daughter decided she wanted to learn on her own. My wife was in the other room and heard a boom. She came running into the living room to see my daughter sitting on the floor on the opposite side of the room. She had stuck a nail in the light socket, and she was literally thrown to the other side of the room by the electricity. We are grateful God spared her life that day. Needless to say, my daughter never walked by or looked at an electrical outlet in the same way. She never had another desire to touch or toy with them, for the lesson was forever engrained within her.

And failures, no matter how big or small, can be great teachers in your life. Sometimes He allows us to fall on our faces so that we will look up to Him. Other times God allows us to fall so that we can learn and move forward. Determine you will learn whatever lesson God has for you through the experience of failure. You do not have to become bitter at God, at others, or even at yourself. You can find the value from the lesson, learn, and move forward to become a better person later down the road.

Get experience to help others.

Your failure was most likely painful, but it does not have to be in vain. Second Corinthians 1:3-4 says that God comforts us so that we may comfort others. You don't need to be comforted if there are no obstacles and failures you've been through. It's only after you've gone through the fire that you need to be comforted. But once God has comforted you, it will open your eyes to other people who have been through similar situations and need to be comforted as well.

This is how it has worked in our lives. When my wife lost a baby late in her pregnancy, we were devastated; but then God began to show us how many other people had been through the same situation. When we were robbed at gunpoint, felt betrayed by people we worked with, were criticized by others, were lied about, and made fun of, we thought it was the end of our ministry and lives. But God has used every one of these situations to allow us to minister and help others. I have met people who have been sexually abused, addicted to nasty drugs, and rejected by family because of their faith in Christ. They would've never chosen those difficulties in their lives, but God turned it for their good so these people could turn around and help others. So whether you think you've failed because of your own choices or because God allowed it to happen that way, realize that

God can use your experiences to encourage, strengthen, comfort, and help others.

Place barriers for the next time.

No one wants to repeat a failure just for the sake of repeating it, so be wise and set barriers in place to help you avoid future failures. Set up accountability, habits, or a restructure of your life so you don't fall into the same pit. Proverbs 22:3 and 27:12 both say that a prudent man foresees the evil and hides himself. A prudent man is a wise and well-advised man. He knows his weaknesses and is cautious to look ahead. Life has taught him lessons, so he chooses to look and avoid pitfalls so that failure is unable to wrap its tentacles around him and squeeze away his life. Learn from the prudent man. Become the prudent man. If you know failure is around the corner, then walk a different path to work.

Get back up.

Proverbs 24:16 says that a just man falls seven times but rises again. Your strength is not measured by what knocks you down. Your strength is seen when you get back up again after you have fallen. Some of the greatest men in history and in the Bible have fallen and failed, but they decided to not stay down, but rather to get back up. Failure is not final, so don't let it keep you down. Psalms 37:24 says that, though a good man falls, he shall not be cast down because the Lord upholds him with His hand. Jump back up, for God is not finished with you yet! Don't stay down, there's much to live for and many reasons to continue and not quit. There's a God who still loves you, people who still need you, and rewards to still work towards. Think about all those that have invested in you, think of your responsibilities, think of those watching you, and the great God in Heaven who has plans for you. It is not easy to get back up, but it's the right thing to do, so don't quit! Let me share with you a poem that was written in the 1800's by John Greenleaf Whittier, yet is still very applicable today.

"YOU MUST NOT QUIT"

When things go wrong, as they sometimes will
When the road you're trudging seems all uphill,
When funds are low and the debts are high,
And you want to smile but you have to sigh.
When troubles are pressing you down a bit,
Rest if you must, but don't you quit.
Success is failure turned inside out,
The silver tint of the clouds of doubt,
And you can never tell how close you are,
It may be near when it seems afar;
So stay in the fight when you're hardest hit,
It's when things seem worst that you mustn't quit.
Change your attitude.

In the introduction of this book, I shared how my dad would correct me every time I said the phrase "I can't." It was more than simply changing the vocabulary I used. Although I do think that was part of it, my dad was teaching me a life lesson. Every time I said, "I can't" about anything, my dad wanted me to know that I really could if I would just put my heart and mind to it. Whether it was playing a sport, working around the house, or even trying to get better grades, my dad taught me that I really could do it if I would stop saying, "I can't." Words reveal beliefs, and beliefs control actions. If you want to press forward and continue after failure, then quit saying, "I can't," and start believing you can. Change your attitude and you will change your failures into triumphs.

Work harder.

I use to envy the person who was smart and didn't have to study, or the person who was naturally talented at a sport or job, but I really don't any more. Since I didn't have the height to be a great defender in basketball, the weight to knock everyone down in football, or the brains to make it on the honor roll, it meant I had to work twice as hard. Putting forth twice the effort never hurt me; in fact, it helped me learn to get back up when I fell down. Everyone will fail at something in life, and most likely it will not be easy to bounce back and recover, but if you're willing to work twice as hard, you can and will regain the lost ground. Sadly, the guy with money, brains, and talent will most likely not be willing to work hard and bounce back once he faces failure. If you're willing to be a scrapper and work hard, no failure will be able to hold you down.

Let's close out this chapter thinking about the old hymn entitled "Let Him Have His Way with Thee." Life has a way of throwing wrenches in our plans and on our path. All have or will meet failure, but cheer up because God still has beautiful plans for you. God's part is already taken care of; your part is to be yielded, to be surrendered, and to let Him have His way in your life.

Would you live for Jesus, and be always pure and good?
Would you walk with Him within the narrow road?
Would you have Him bear your burden, carry all your load?
Let Him have His way with thee.

His pow'r can make you what you ought to be;
His blood can cleanse your heart and make you free;
His love can fill your soul, and you will see
'Twas best for Him to have His way with thee.
Would you in His kingdom find a place of constant rest?
Would you prove Him true in providential test?
Would you in His service labor always at your best?
Let Him have His way with thee.

His pow'r can make you what you ought to be;
His blood can cleanse your heart and make you free;
His love can fill your soul, and you will see
'Twas best for Him to have His way with thee.

Chapter 16

OVERCOMING CONTROL ISSUES

Many people like being in control, and regrettably, I'm included in this list. For example, I like to drive the vehicle, because I know when it's time to speed up, take it easy, hit the brakes, get in another lane, stop for a coffee, or keep on the road to get to my destination. For you, it might be wanting control of the TV remote, the car radio, or your schedule. Being in control of areas makes one feel in charge, confident, and at ease. There's no harm in taking control of personal areas, but control freaks know no limits and end up running over anyone in their way. Releasing control is not easy, but it is possible. Relationships are strained, if not destroyed, because of control issues. Here's a few suggestions to help you overcome control.

Learn to trust others.

Not everyone may do things exactly like you do, but you have to learn to trust others. If you think you are the only one who can do something right, your actions are actually belittling to others. For example, if you redo the same chore after your child folds laundry, makes a bed, or sweeps the floor, your actions are saying that you really don't trust your child. No one wants to be with someone who thinks they know it all or are better than everyone else. Learn to trust others and relinquish control before you begin losing friends and hurting those closest to you. By allowing others to be in charge, you are proving that you trust them, and you know they can do the job well.

Trust is difficult for most people, but you must understand that strong relationships do not exist without trust. When talking about the characteristics of a virtuous woman, Proverbs 31:11 says, "The heart of her husband doth safely trust in her." When trust leaves a relationship, the relationship dwindles and soon dies. A controlling person may say they cannot trust others, but the end result is destruction of relationships. If you want to keep relationships, you must learn to trust others. You must learn to think positively about others, knowing they are not out to hurt you or that they hate you. Trusting others will allow you to both build strong relationships as well as release control.

Another reason it may be hard to trust others is because of unrealistic expectations. If you expect perfection, no one or no thing will ever satisfy you. A good rule of thumb is to remember that relationships are always more important than the task in front of you. If you place the job above the person, you will stay frustrated and be unable to trust others. Drop the perfectionism and you will be able to trust. Learn to trust and you will be less controlling.

Realize God knows better than you.

Romans 8:28 teaches us that all things work together for good to them that love God. God truly does know best. You cannot always control sickness, bad influence, criticisms, other's actions, or a child falling down. Although you want to be cautious, you have to trust when it comes to most things in life. Do you know that God can protect you, provide for you, and wants the best for you? It's one thing to say you believe it, but do you back that belief up by letting God work? I have been guilty of telling God He has control over my life yet then grabbing the steering wheel when I don't feel like things are headed in the direction I think is best. Sadly, many times God doesn't fight for the driver's seat in our lives; rather, He lets us make decisions. You have to voluntarily let God navigate your life, knowing that He knows and wants what is best for you.

When Job worried that his kids might be living differently than he wanted and than God had commanded, he woke up and spoke to God, requesting God to forgive and keep them from evil (Job 1:5). Instead of trying to control every area of his children's lives, he took it to the God who could penetrate hearts. When a parent, spouse, friend, or spiritual leader attempts to police the details of someone else's life, it usually only infuriates the person instead of making it better. The control must be relinquished and given over to God, for He knows what's best for you and for them.

What's the real reason?

There's usually a reason that someone feels the need to control. Is it because someone failed you in the past? Is it because you were treated poorly and never allowed to make decisions in the past? Whatever the reason is, you need to identify it in order to overcome it. Remember that you cannot change the past. Trying to relive the past by controlling the present will only make you miserable, not change what previously happened. Ask God to forgive you for holding onto bad feelings of the past and allow Him to take control as He deems best.

Control can also be rooted in pride, believing everything is all about you. Since pride is focused on self, you are sure to hurt others. God resists the proud but gives grace to the humble (James 4:6, 1 Peter 5:5). Pride is offensive to God and to others, so bury the pride and you will be greatly helped.

Lastly, control can be rooted in fear. Perhaps it could be fear of what you may lose if you don't control the situation. It might be fear that you won't look good, or even that you'll lose that person in your life. Since there's no fear in love (1 John 4:8), decide to release the control and opt for love. Love God and let God's love work through you, for He knows what's best for your life.

Accept that you can be wrong.

The person who loves control usually feels as if they are seldom wrong. As a result of not being wrong, they refuse to accept blame.

It seems everyone can see the error except for the controller. This does not gain friends, influence, or love. In fact, it's a characteristic that causes the controller to become a lonely person. Just accept the fact that you're not perfect, that you could be wrong, and that others might have a better opinion or better way of doing things than you do. If you can't accept blame, people will quit talking. Not because they think you are getting better, but because they know you are too stubborn to listen to them. When you think you're always right, the only one you are fooling is yourself.

Let's close out this chapter meditating on the old hymn entitled "Is Your All on the Altar?" For someone who likes control, this song hits a nerve. The words and the message are very powerful!

You have longed for sweet peace,
And for faith to increase,
And have earnestly, fervently prayed;
But you cannot have rest,
Or be perfectly blest,
Until all on the altar is laid.

Is your all on the altar of sacrifice laid?
Your heart does the Spirit control?
You can only be blest,
And have peace and sweet rest,
As you yield Him your body and soul.

Chapter 17

OVERCOMING WORRY

No one wants to worry, yet many live their lives as if they do. There are so many reasons to make someone worried, which in turn makes one miserable. When someone lives in worry, they miss out on the blessings of now, and are prey to a gloomy outlook on life. God created the world perfectly, placing Adam and Eve in the garden. The moment man sinned, everything changed. Thorns, death, sweat, and worry all crept into the picture, and they haven't left man's side since then. Death and sweat remain, but just as one can clear the land that's covered in thorns, so you can clear your life from worries.

Filter your news.

When my family and I served as missionaries in Argentina, we made a decision in our household to not watch the local news. I know this may sound extreme, closed-minded, and ignorant to you, but news in our city was much more crude than news when I was growing up. The news channel would show the corpse of a person that was in a vehicular accident, an elderly couple killed in a robbery, or highlight the most recent rapists or thieves in the area. Local news seemed to be more of a fear-inducing gossip channel. My young daughters didn't need to see that, and my wife and I didn't need to think about it.

I realize no one can or should live in a bubble, but we must also be cautious to filter the information we permit to enter into our minds, houses, and families. Since our mind usually focuses more quickly on the negative rather than on the positive, we should be selective of what we welcome into our lives. Whether it's a newspaper, news channel, neighborhood discussions, or friend's comments, you must filter what you dwell on. Knowing or not knowing news doesn't change reality, but it does change perception. If you feed your mind with that which makes you worry, you will stress yourself to the point where you don't want to leave your house. Filter the information you allow into your life and you will worry less.

Share it with someone.

Bottling something up doesn't help; it usually ends in a future explosion. I am grateful that I have a wife, a pastor, and great friends with whom I can share my burdens, concerns, and worries, but I also have an all-wise and all-powerful God with whom I can share them. God tells me to cast all my cares (worries, concerns, anxieties) upon Him because He cares for me (1 Peter 5:7). God wants you to share your burdens with Him, and by doing so you can quit carrying the worries by yourself. There's no reason to walk around worried if you will simply share these worries with the One who is powerful enough to take care of them.

Do what you can and don't worry about what you can't control.

Most worries have to do with the past or the future, things we can't change even if we wanted to. If you can change something, then by all means change it, but if it's out of your control then your worries are in vain. You can't add a hair to your head or an inch to your stature. You can't change who occupies the presidency, the family God has given you, or the gender God has made you. Work hard to change what's in your power (your work ethic, your attitude, or your own happiness), and learn to quit worrying about what is not in your power.

Leave it in God's hands.

This is much easier said than done; nevertheless, it is very important. Once you have done all you can in an area, you must trust God to do the rest. For example, once your children are out of the house, pray that they do right and commend them to God's care. If you went to the doctor and are told that you or a loved one has a sickness, you have to ask God for His grace and leave it in His hands. When you truly believe God knows best and wants the best for you, then you have to leave it in His hands. Of course, you will think about it and be tempted to worry about it every hour or day; but you must, once again, tell yourself that it is out of your hands and in God's. Learning to tell yourself that God has this and that He is going to take care of it, will help you with your worries. If you don't tell yourself, no one else can tell you either. In the Bible, as Paul was leaving the Christians to go to Jerusalem, he told them he was commending them to God (Acts 20:32). Paul was no longer going to be able to preach to them, pray with them, help them, or counsel them, so he turned them over to God. And you must learn this same lesson. Once something is out of your control, then commend it to God, knowing that He is stronger, wiser, and more capable than you are.

Change your focus.

Almost everyone has heard or knows the story of David and Goliath. The young shepherd who takes down the warrior giant. But the interesting thing about the story is that King Saul, his son Jonathan, and the entire Israeli army was also present that day. They were ready to go to war until they saw the giant walk out. Everyone cowered, and no one was willing to die at the hands of the giant. When David spoke up, his brothers mocked him, the king mocked him, and the giant mocked him. "David is a dead man," was the thought of everyone who was looking at the fight that day. But they were all missing something. David was not focused on the stature of the giant, he was focused on the strength of his God. David didn't see this fight, or even his life for that matter, with the same eyes everyone else was using. David's focus was on God, and God had never lost a battle up to that date.

You and I would be wise to take notes from David. Your worries are small in the shadow of our great God. Are you worried God cannot handle your problems or that He will fail you? Has God ever abandoned you or failed you in the past? Are God's promises not good for today? If God is still alive, on the throne, and faithful to keep His promises, then the problem does not lie with God. Maybe it's time to change the focus from the problems of life to the power of God. God is greater, stronger, and more powerful, so place your focus on Him. When your focus changes, your worries will diminish.

Quit comparing.

We live in a social media-driven world. You can see and know about people you went to school with twenty years ago or friends that live hundreds of miles away. While there are great advantages to social media, there are great disadvantages as well. Of those disadvantages, jealousy and comparison have to be near the top. You can see what others ate, where they vacationed, who they visited, and all the glamorous aspects that they want to show. You might say, "one should rejoice with those that rejoice," but the honest truth is that we want the life of others and to be happy like everyone else is. This comparison becomes unhealthy and makes us live in misery, along with all those close to us. And because we want the portrayed happiness everyone else has, we live worrying that our lives don't match up to everyone else's.

What Jesus said to Peter as they were walking down the road seems very applicable today. Jesus was telling Peter about his future, and all of a sudden, Peter asked Jesus about John, saying, "Lord, and what shall this man do?" (John 21:21) Jesus could have told him that he would see, or it wasn't time to know, but instead He told Peter, "What is that to thee? follow thou me." (John 21:22) In essence, Jesus told him to not worry about John, just to do what he knew was right and follow Him. Wow! Today we walk around questioning why God would let someone act like that, live like that, not have any problems, and apparently have everything in their lives. But we should learn what Peter learned that day: quit worrying about everyone else and live your life for God like you should.

Think on the promises.

God has given His children so many exceedingly great and precious promises (2 Peter 1:4). Next time you begin to worry, start looking up, listing, and rehearsing God's promises out loud or in your heart. Here's a few to think on:

- God will never, never leave you. — Hebrews 13:5; Isaiah 49:15
- God will never stop loving you. — Romans 8:38-39
- God has wonderful thoughts of you and plans for you. — Jeremiah 29:11; 1 Corinthians 2:9
- God wants to hear from you. — Hebrews 4:16
- God no longer remembers your sins. — Psalm 103:12; Isaiah 43:25; Hebrews 8:12; Colossians 2:17

- God wants to give you rest. — Matthew 11:28-30

Let's close out this chapter meditating on the old hymn entitled "It Is Well with My Soul." When you're worried, just remember that God can make all things well.

When peace, like a river, attendeth my way,
When sorrows like sea billows roll;
Whatever my lot, Thou hast taught me to say,
It is well, it is well with my soul.
It is well with my soul,
It is well, it is well with my soul.
Though Satan should buffet, though trials should come,
Let this blest assurance control,
That Christ hath regarded my helpless estate,
And hath shed His own blood for my soul.
It is well with my soul,
It is well, it is well with my soul.

Conclusion

In the last book of the Bible, Revelation, the future is unfolded for us. Check out what Revelation 17:14 says: "These shall make war with the Lamb, and the Lamb shall overcome them: for he is Lord of lords, and King of kings: and they that are with him are called, and chosen, and faithful."

The clear conclusions we can derive are two-fold: first, the devil and his followers are always at war with our Lord. And last, the Lord always overcomes. Our God never loses! He's an overcomer! And according to 1 John 5:4, all those that follow our Lord are overcomers as well. There is no passion, practice, or person that should make a child of God quit or give up. You, dear friend, are an overcomer! Don't allow the devil to keep you in bonds. It's time to break free and live in the victory God has intended for you.

Bibliography

Chapter 1 — Overcoming Fear

Page 3 — Definition of fear is from page 2161 of The Century Dictionary, 1911 and is a public domain dictionary

Page 3 — Acronym for "F. E. A. R." is claimed to originate from Neale Donald Walsch

Page 5 — The Pilgrim's Progress, 1678, is a Christian allegory written by John Bunyan.

Page 9 — Hymn "What a Friend We Have in Jesus" by Joseph M. Scriven, 1855. Copyright status is public domain.

Page 10 — The two quotes comes from the book Fear Not by Segun T. Obadimu

Page 15 — Hymn "Living by Faith" written by James Wells, 1918. Copyright status is public domain.

Page 15-16 — Hymn at the end "Follow On" by William O. Cushing, 1878. Copyright status is public domain.

Chapter 2 — Overcoming Pessimism

Page 17 — "85% of people hate the job they are currently doing" Gallup poll from June 2017

Page 20 — Rhinoceros Success by Scott Alexander. Copyright 1980. Spot Light Publishers, Inc.

Page 24 — Hymn at the end "Count Your Blessings" by Johnson Oatman, Jr., 1897. Copyright status is public domain.

Chapter 3 — Overcoming Grief

Page 31-32 — Hymn at the end "Farther Along" by W. B. Stevens, 1911. Copyright status is public domain.

Chapter 4 — Overcoming Temptation

Page 37 — quote from A Man Called Peter (1951) chapter 4

Page 42 — quote from the book Tempted and Tried by Russell Moore; Crossway Books 2011

Page 43 — Hymn at the end "Yield Not to Temptation" by Horatio R. Palmer, 1868. Copyright status is public domain.

Chapter 5 — Overcoming Anger

Page 51 — Hymn at the end "Turn Your Eyes upon Jesus" by Helen H. Lemmel, 1922. Copyright status is public domain.

Chapter 6 — Overcoming Loneliness

Page 56 — Denis E. Waitley is an American motivational speaker, writer and consultant born in 1933

Page 57-58 — Hymn at the end "What a Friend We Have in Jesus" by Joseph M. Scriven, 1855. Copyright status is public domain.

Chapter 7 — Overcoming Pride

Page 64 — quote by Ken Blanchard. He's an American author, business consultant and motivational speaker. 1939 to present day (2021)

Page 65 — Hymn at the end "I Need Thee Every Hour" Annie S. Hawks, 1872. Copyright status is public domain.

Chapter 8 — Overcoming Laziness

Page 70-71 — Hymn at the end "Work, for the Night Is Coming" by Anna L. Coghill, 1854. Copyright status is public domain.

Chapter 9 — Overcoming Stagnation

Page 75 —The movie Sheffey. Robert Sayers Sheffey (1820-1902) was an American Methodist evangelist and circuit-riding preacher.

Page 77-78 — Hymn at the end "I Gave My Life for Thee" by Frances R. Havergal, 1858. Copyright status is public domain.

Chapter 10 — Overcoming Bad Habits

Page 81-82 Hymn at the end "I Surrender All" by Judson W. Van DeVenter, 1896. Copyright status is public domain.

Chapter 11 — Overcoming Victimhood

Page 89 — Hymn at the end "I Shall Not Be Moved" by Alfred Henry Ackley, 1908. Copyright status is public domain.

Chapter 12 — Overcoming Doubt

Page 99 — Hymn at the end "All the Way My Savior Leads Me" by Frances J. Crosby, 1875. Copyright status is public domain.

Chapter 13 — Overcoming Ungratefulness

Page 105-106 — Hymn at the end "Revive Us Again" by William P. Mackay, 1863. Copyright status is public domain.

Chapter 14 — Overcoming Depression

Page 110-111 — Quote by Dale Carnegie, American businessman and writer. (1888-1955)

Page 112-113 — Hymn at the end "I Must Tell Jesus" by Elisha A. Hoffman, 1893. Copyright status is public domain.

Chapter 15 — Overcoming Failure

Page 119 — Poem Don't Quit by John Greenleaf Whittier (1807-1892),

Page 121 — Hymn at the end "Let Him Have His Way with Thee" by Cyrus S. Nusbaum, 1898. Copyright status is public domain.

Chapter 16 — Overcoming Control Issues Worry

Page 127 — Hymn at the end "Is Your All on the Altar?" by Elisha A. Hoffman, 1900. Copyright status is public domain.

Chapter 17 — Overcoming Worry

Page 135 — Hymn at the end "It Is Well with My Soul" by Horatio G. Spafford, 1873. Copyright status is public domain.

Other Books by the Author

Leadership Opposite

The Bible is the most accurate and proven Book of all times. It is in the Bible where we find out about life, work, marriage, friendship, money, and love. God teaches about every subject, and leadership is certainly one. We see leadership taught clearly by way of principle, command, and example. Yet God's way of doing things is not always how we would guess or imagine. In God's economy, to be greatest is to be servant, to live is to die, to receive is to give... seems opposite of what we would think in our finite minds.

In *Leadership Opposite*, you will discover what may seem to go against the grain of normal leadership, but these tried and proven principles are God's way to lead.

Building a Team

Teams are great, and so much can be attained with a team. However, on the flip side, it is not always easy to work in a team. Whether you serve as the leader of the team or as a player on the team, you can be key in making your team better and more affective. Everyone wants the benefits of a team, but very few work hard to the point in which they can receive them. The goal of this book is to share basic and simple insights that make teams effective.

They Turned the World Upside Down

A 71-day devotional based upon the lives of common people who transformed the world in which they lived. The stories of those who served in mission will inspire you to live on mission wherever God has placed you!

Thiving In Life

We are in a spiritual warfare. We are not fighting against people or things we can physically see. Our fight is not against flesh and blood according to Ephesians 6:12. I am convinced that the battleground of the devil is mainly in our head. Many people get discouraged, bitter, hurt, upset, frustrated, depressed, and pretty much give up on life. Yes, they can still breathe and walk but they are somewhat paralyzed and not able to advance. These attitudes show up in the fact that they have a bad marriage, can't make friends, shelter themselves, quit believing and in general just want to quit. If we can adjust our thinking, we can improve our living.

Basic Etiquette for Leaders

As we relate to the people around us, we should do so with the most respect. This book is laid out in such a way as to represent a normal day: walking through the rooms of your house, the workplace, church and just out and about. I hope this will serve as a kind reminder to show others that they truly do matter to you.

Making Your Marriage Great Again

Marriage is one of the greatest institutions ever created by God, but the devil wants to make it one of the worst. Marriage is where you can experience the greatest happiness, success and fun, but sadly most marriages experience only disappointments, frustration and pain. Don't just endure your marriage; enjoy your marriage once again!

A Memoir of Miracles

As a newly married couple on deputation Jeff and Mindy read many missionary biographies about men and women of the past. They believed that God is still working miracles on mission fields all around the world, and years later they wrote this book to share some of the amazing things God did in their lives while serving as missionaries in Argentina. Their desire is that young people would read these stories and realize that God can use them today in a great way.

Vicotry Over Porn

The devil is a professional assassin and has his crosshairs specifically on those trying to serve God with their lives. He uses discouragement, pride and greed on many people, but we believe that one of his choice weapons in our day and age is pornography. Many good men and women have fallen prey to the snares of this easy-accessible, oneclick-away-promise of fulfillment. Most that fall into the grips of pornography want to get out but feel trapped. This book will point you to truly having victory over porn. God does not want anyone to live as a slave to sin. Break free and find the victory that Christ has for you!

Missions Conference Manual

The only prayer request that our Lord Jesus Christ expressed when He was on this earth was for more laborers (Matthew 9:37-38). Many good missionaries are retiring, and we are in dire need of more laborers to get to the mission field before our Lord's soon return. This small booklet offers suggestions, ideas, and tools on how to have the best missions conference ever!

If you would like to order these or many other books, visit www.bcwe.org/ogpublishing, email jeff@visionmissions.com, write to Our Generation Publishing, PO Box 442, Alpharetta, GA 30009, or call 770-456-5881.

Our Generation Publishing is an effort of the Babptist Center for World Evangelism, Vision Baptist Missions, and the Our Generation Training Center to bring resources to churches and individuals to further the cause of Christ in world evangelism. Through Our Generation Publishing you will find these and many other resources that, prayerfully, God can use in your life and ministry to reach the world with the Gospel in our generation.